SOCIAL ISSUES
FIRSTHAND

Date and Acquaintance Rape

Other Books in the Social Issues Firsthand Series:

Date and
Acquaintance Rape

Sharon R. Gunton, Book Editor

GREENHAVEN PRESS
A part of Gale, Cengage Learning

GALE
CENGAGE Learning

Detroit • New York • San Francisco • New Haven, Conn • Waterville, Maine • London

Christine Nasso, *Publisher*
Elizabeth Des Chenes, *Managing Editor*

© 2009 Greenhaven Press, a part of Gale, Cengage Learning.

Gale and Greenhaven Press are registered trademarks used herein under license.

For more information, contact:
Greenhaven Press
27500 Drake Rd.
Farmington Hills, MI 48331-3535
Or you can visit our Internet site at gale.cengage.com

For product information and technology assistance, contact us at

Gale Customer Support, 1-800-877-4253
For permission to use material from this text or product, submit all requests online at www.cengage.com/permissions

Further permissions questions can be emailed to permissionrequest@cengage.com

Articles in Greenhaven Press anthologies are often edited for length to meet page requirements. In addition, original titles of these works are changed to clearly present the main thesis and to explicitly indicate the author's opinion. Every effort is made to ensure that Greenhaven Press accurately reflects the original intent of the authors. Every effort has been made to trace the owners of copyrighted material.

Cover image copyright Andrija Kovac, 2008. Used under license from shutterstock.com.

LIBRARY OF CONGRESS CATALOGING-IN-PUBLICATION DATA

Date and acquaintance rape / Sharon R. Gunton, book editor.
p. cm. -- (Social issues firsthand)
Includes bibliographical references and index.
ISBN 978-0-7377-4250-3 (hardcover)
1. Date rape. 2. Date rape--Prevention. 3. Acquaintance rape. 4. Acquaintance rape-- Prevention. I. Gunton, Sharon.
HV6561.D34 2009
362.883--dc22

2008020683

Printed in the United States of America
1 2 3 4 5 6 7 12 11 10 09 08

Contents

Foreword

Social issues are often viewed in abstract terms. Pressing challenges such as poverty, homelessness, and addiction are viewed as problems to be defined and solved. Politicians, social scientists, and other experts engage in debates about the extent of the problems, their causes, and how best to remedy them. Often overlooked in these discussions is the human dimension of the issue. Behind every policy debate over poverty, homelessness, and substance abuse, for example, are real people struggling to make ends meet, to survive life on the streets, and to overcome addiction to drugs and alcohol. Their stories are ubiquitous and compelling. They are the stories of everyday people—perhaps your own family members or friends—and yet they rarely influence the debates taking place in state capitols, the national Congress, or the courts.

The disparity between the public debate and private experience of social issues is well illustrated by looking at the topic of poverty. Each year the U.S. Census Bureau establishes a poverty threshold. A household with an income below the threshold is defined as poor, while a household with an income above the threshold is considered able to live on a basic subsistence level. For example, in 2003 a family of two was considered poor if its income was less than $12,015; a family of four was defined as poor if its income was less than $18,810. Based on this system, the bureau estimates that 35.9 million Americans (12.5 percent of the population) lived below the poverty line in 2003, including 12.9 million children below the age of eighteen.

Commentators disagree about what these statistics mean. Social activists insist that the huge number of officially poor Americans translates into human suffering. Even many families that have incomes above the threshold, they maintain, are likely to be struggling to get by. Other commentators insist that the statistics exaggerate the problem of poverty in the United States. Compared to people in developing countries, they point out, most so-called poor families have a high quality of life. As stated by journalist Fidelis Iyebote, "Cars are owned by 70 percent of 'poor' households.... Color televisions belong to 97 percent of the 'poor' [and] videocassette recorders belong to nearly 75 percent.... Sixty-four percent have microwave ovens, half own a stereo system, and over a quarter possess an automatic dishwasher."

However, this debate over the poverty threshold and what it means is likely irrelevant to a person living in poverty. Simply put, poor people do not need the government to tell them whether they are poor. They can see it in the stack of bills they cannot pay. They are aware of it when they are forced to choose between paying rent or buying food for their children. They become painfully conscious of it when they lose their homes and are forced to live in their cars or on the streets. Indeed, the written stories of poor people define the meaning of poverty more vividly than a government bureaucracy could ever hope to. Narratives composed by the poor describe losing jobs due to injury or mental illness, depict horrific tales of childhood abuse and spousal violence, recount the loss of friends and family members. They evoke the slipping away of social supports and government assistance, the descent into substance abuse and addiction, the harsh realities of life on the streets. These are the perspectives on poverty that are too often omitted from discussions over the extent of the problem and how to solve it.

Greenhaven Press's *Social Issues Firsthand* series provides a forum for the often-overlooked human perspectives on society's most divisive topics of debate. Each volume focuses on one social issue and presents a collection of ten to sixteen narratives by those who have had personal involvement with the topic. Extra care has been taken to include a diverse range of perspectives. For example, in the volume on adoption, readers will find the stories of birth parents who have made an adoption plan, adoptive parents, and adoptees themselves. After exposure to these varied points of view, the reader will have a clearer understanding that adoption is an intense, emotional experience full of joyous highs and painful lows for all concerned.

The debate surrounding embryonic stem cell research illustrates the moral and ethical pressure that the public brings to bear on the scientific community. However, while nonexperts often criticize scientists for not considering the potential negative impact of their work, ironically the public's reaction against such discoveries can produce harmful results as well. For example, although the outcry against embryonic stem cell research in the United States has resulted in fewer embryos being destroyed, those with Parkinson's, such as actor Michael J. Fox, have argued that prohibiting the development of new stem cell lines ultimately will prevent a timely cure for the disease that is killing Fox and thousands of others.

Each book in the series contains several features that enhance its usefulness, including an in-depth introduction, an annotated table of contents, bibliographies for further research, a list of organizations to contact, and a thorough index. These elements—combined with the poignant voices of people touched by tragedy and triumph—make the Social Issues Firsthand series a valuable resource for research on today's topics of political discussion.

Introduction

Author Marge Piercy wrote "Circles on the Water," a powerful poem in which she says: "There is no difference between being raped/And going headfirst through a windshield/Except that afterward you are afraid not of cars/But half the human race."

In the case of date rape, there is fear *and* distrust—someone familiar, even beloved, has acted in a hurtful way, inflicting tremendous emotional and physical harm. Additionally, victims who have been drugged then sexually assaulted face confusion about what has happened to them. When drugs are slipped into the food or drinks of unsuspecting victims, they become so incapacitated that they often are unaware that they are being raped, or have no strength or presence of mind to defend themselves, as if it were happening in some awful dream.

The Date-Rape Drugs

Any drug used to facilitate sexual assault can be considered a predatory drug, including marijuana, street drugs, club drugs like ecstasy, and over-the-counter or prescription drugs like sleeping pills. Three notable club drugs used by sexual predators are ketamine hydrochloride, Rohypnol (or roofies), and gamma hydroxybutyrate (GHB).

But what is the most common date rape drug of all? A 1999 article in *Cosmopolitan* magazine titled "The Date-Rape Drug You Take Yourself" cites a 1989 study revealing that three out of four women who were sexually assaulted had been drinking alcohol at the time of the occurrence. Quoting the chief of sex crimes prosecution for the Manhattan, New York, district attorney's office, the article explains the dangers of alcohol consumption. It impairs judgment, makes victims weaker and less able to fight their assailants, and makes it harder for a person to figure out how to get out of a dangerous situation and remember enough to convince a jury later. Also, alcohol can intensify the effects of other predatory drugs, making them more powerful and dangerous.

Laws Against Predatory Drugs

Congress passed the Drug-Induced Rape Prevention and Punishment Act in 1996. According to a memo from the Office of the Attorney General, the act gives courts the right to confer "criminal penalties of up to twenty years imprisonment for any person who distributes a controlled substance, such as Rohypnol, to a person with the intent to commit a crime of violence, including rape."

In 2000, President Bill Clinton signed into law a bill bearing the names of two young women who were victims of the predatory drug GHB. The Hillory J. Farias and Samantha Reid Date-Rape Drug Prohibition Act of 2000 classifies GHB as a Schedule I substance, the same tightly regulated category as heroin. Those found possessing, manufacturing, or distributing the drug can be sentenced to up to twenty years in prison.

Death by GHB

In the early morning hours of January 17, 1999, Samantha Reid slipped into a coma after drinking a soda laced with gamma hydroxybutyrate. GHB acts on the nervous system as a depressant or anesthesia. It once was available in stores and on the Internet for use as muscle enhancer, but was banned in the United States in 1990 because of problems users had experienced. It is now made illegally and not manufactured in standard dosages; consequently, the potency of the drug can vary wildly. It has a slightly salty taste, is odorless, and looks exactly like water.

The details of Samantha's drugging involve a sequence of events that began with typical teenage socializing, moved into reckless and dangerous behavior, followed by fear, panic, delayed action, and lifelong consequences for everyone involved.

The facts as reported in the *Detroit News* on December 5, 1999, were as follows: On January 16, 1999, Samantha, her friend Melanie, and Melanie's stepsister went for a ride with Daniel and Nicholas, two seniors from their high school, who took them to an apartment to watch a movie. At the apartment, they met another young man named Joshua, who laced Samantha's and Melanie's drinks with GHB because, as he stated later in court, he felt it would loosen them up and make the gathering more fun. Both girls began vomiting within minutes and passed out. The three men, afraid and thinking perhaps the girls would "sleep it off," didn't take them to the hospital until almost three hours later. Samantha died the next day, at the age of fifteen.

Joshua had acquired the drug from the twenty-five-year-old owner of the apartment, who had bought it on the street. The girls' reaction to the drug was not really surprising. Although Rohypnol was often in the press in the 1990s, GHB soon became recognized as an even more dangerous drug because, unlike Rohypnol, it is manufactured illegally. As a result, the potency of GHB is completely unpredictable and its use—even in very small amounts—can bring horrible, unforeseeable consequences. Trinka Porrata, founder of Project GHB, Inc., has stated: "The risk of dying is so volatile and unpredictable. . . . It is the most dangerous drug I have dealt with in twenty-five years." At the time of the *Detroit News* article, she said that, from 1995 to 1999, at least forty-six reported deaths and more than 5,500 reported overdoses had been linked to GHB across the nation. She thought the actual figures were probably much higher.

Samantha's life ended needlessly and tragically. But the lives of the perpetrators also changed profoundly. When the trial concerning Samantha's death was over, they faced guilty verdicts of involuntary manslaughter and lesser poisoning charges; their sentences could be as long as twenty years of incarceration.

Avoid Being a Victim

As Samantha's story shows, these drugs can be slipped into any food or drink. But most commonly they are used at parties and clubs, where low light, noise, crowds, and alcohol use makes suspicious behavior less likely to be detected. Leaving a drink unattended is always risky, as is drinking from punch bowls, pitchers, and tubs. It is better to get a drink directly from the bartender rather than a waitress and watch the bartender mix the drink. If drugging is suspected, getting to a hospital immediately is essential. Also, most hospitals do not automatically test for drugs, so it is important to ask to be tested.

There are paper coasters and strips that can detect the presence of GHB and ketamine. The paper turns a color when a few drops of a spiked drink are placed on a coaster or strip. Many colleges and universities have made the test papers available to students; some have put the coasters in kits for incoming students. But these paper gauges are not foolproof. They are hard to read in dark places or when a colored drink is put on them. And because there are so many other date-rape drugs that can be used, testing for two of them is hardly a perfect solution. Experts differ on many points when they discuss predatory drugs, but in one instance they all agree: the most effective way to avoid being victimized is extreme caution.

Social Issues Firsthand: Date and Acquaintance Rape presents personal narratives about the issue from a number of perspectives, focusing on the cultural influences that lead to rape, surviving date rape, and preventing further abuse. The following viewpoints demonstrate the sensitive nature of the subject and provide catalysts for further discussion.

CHAPTER 1

The Culture of Rape

The Sexual Assault Culture on Campus

Leslie Campis

Leslie Campis is the director of sexual assault response and edu-cation services at Emory University in Atlanta, Georgia. She found that when she compared her own college experiences with those of current students, there were some notable differences. She says quite pointedly that there is more danger now and re-fers to "the culture that enables sexual assault on campuses." In her article, she delineates her observations concerning the com-plex factors that have led to a serious challenge for young adults.

As I sat before an array of interested and disengaged faces, it occurred to me that a benefit of middle age was that I had a historical perspective to offer that was, for the young women in my audience, wholly new. "When I was in college, women could drink, even pass out on a sofa, and never have to worry about being assaulted," I stated. Looks of surprise bounced at me. Eyes widened questioningly, and one remark burst forth: "That's sad. Why is it so different now?"

I remember feeling as surprised as they looked. In that moment, I realized that their life experience consisted of never knowing a time when it was different. I was speaking with them to raise awareness, and yet I had the clear sense that what I was conveying was a familiar and accepted part of their lives; they already knew my message about the risk of sexual assault in college. These young women revealed to me their resignation at the thought of the horrific statistical probability that one in four of them is likely to be sexually assaulted be-fore graduating, It was unsettling to learn that they had come to think of an unwanted sexual experience as part of college life.

Leslie Campis, "Reflections on a First Year: The Sexual Assault Culture on Campus," *Women's News and Narratives*, fall 2005. Reproduced by permission.

Different Expectations

The question "Why is it so different now?" permeates my thinking as I work to challenge the culture that enables sexual assault on college campuses. As I engage students in discussion of this significant issue, its full complexity has emerged. The larger cultural context of our society has been identified as a "rape culture," with rape myths and stereotypical gender roles contributing to the problem. Certainly, this factor is influential but not fully explanatory. The current generation has different expectations of sexual and romantic relationships, with no rules or guidelines to help them navigate. Today's college students live in a culture of "hooking up, friends with benefits, and booty calls." Relationship options are wide open: it is accepted that men and women can "hook up" with many people with no expectation of commitment. Some students are alienated by the "hook up" culture; some experience it as a way to establish status and power; others are confused by it. One student explained, "If you hook up repeatedly with a guy, it might mean you are starting a relationship." She then checked herself, appeared perplexed, and stated, "That seems kind of backwards, doesn't it?"

Not only is a commonly understood set of expectations regarding relationships absent, but many students come to college having little experience with one-on-one relationships. Groups of friends might spend time together, but individual, personal encounters that might be construed as dating are the exception. Relationships and communications occur through the filter of a computer screen, replacing the testing ground dating relationships provide.

Communication and Consent

A brave male student spoke about his anxiety when attempting to initiate a sexual relationship with a woman. He indicated that by not directly acknowledging his intent and desire, he could ease into the encounter without risking embarrassment or humiliation. Verbalizing sexual interest is something that each gender prefers the other to initiate. The crux of the issue is that no one wants to have the intimate verbal exchange of consent, which ironically feels more personal than the act of sex itself. To ease the anxiety and awkwardness of intimacy, students can turn to alcohol. To further complicate the issue, most students do not know that sex with someone who is too drunk to give consent is rape. One male student struggled with this information, asking, "We drink so we *can* have sex . . . so what are we supposed to do?" It is not surprising, then, that the majority of sexual assaults on college campuses occur between acquaintances when one or both have been drinking. Within this ambiguous "dating" culture, sexual assault is an insidious and pervasive problem.

As I have immersed myself in understanding the college-campus culture, I have learned well its language and practices. To "get in a guy's way" by preventing a sexual conquest is to be a "cockblock"; on the other side, women spread the word about "sketchy" guys to warn their friends; and it is well known that alcohol can be used as a date-rape drug. It is a known practice that some men will encourage a woman to become extremely intoxicated so that the man can have sex with her, regardless of what she wants. Students openly acknowledge this behavior, yet do not consider it to be possible sexual assault. I observe students' struggle with the "hook up" culture, the legal definition of rape, and anxiety about potentially causing harm. "How do you know when she is too drunk to give consent?" is a question I frequently encounter.

Not Recognizing Rape

For women, acquaintance rape is so closely intertwined with normative expectations of campus culture that it is hard sometimes for them even to recognize it. I bear witness to the struggle of victimized women to define their experience. There are many times when women awaken in an unfamiliar place to realize that someone had sex with them, yet they have no memory of it. These young women feel exploited and violated, but they question whether they even have the right to feel that way. Their experience is one they have heard happens to others and should just be attributed to a night of "drunken sex." They may grapple with confusion about whether it was rape or maybe a bad choice for which they should blame themselves. "If we were both drunk, who is to blame?" they might ask.

Perhaps confusion results from the reactions of others. It is difficult to acknowledge feelings of violation when friends say, "That's what happens; don't make a big deal of it" or "What did you expect? You went to his room, so you are to blame." If they confront or question the man, the woman might be told, "You were all over me" and "You wanted to." These women know in their hearts, though, that they never would have consented to sex if given a choice. They do not feel entitled to protest or even to be angry in the current campus culture. It is not surprising that a recent study found that almost half of college women whose experience met the legal definition of rape did not think that they had been raped.

Moving into the Future

So "why is it so different now?" I am not completely certain yet, but I have learned much. Although I am resigned to the fact that rape will not be eliminated on college campuses, I have witnessed that—when given the opportunity—students are eager to engage in dialogue about these issues. They are open to questioning and challenging the pervading cultural acceptance of acquaintance rape. . . .

The desire to explore the boundaries of autonomy, sexuality, and relationships can occur in an environment where acquaintance rape and the use of alcohol as a date-rape drug are no longer tolerated and minimized. To accomplish this end,

we must educate, question, and engage in meaningful dialogue to challenge the campus culture, knowing that it was
not always this way.

What My Fraternity Brothers Taught Me

Sean, as told to Peggy Reeves Sanday

Fraternities are notorious for being the scene of sexual assault and rape, especially gang rape. In her book Fraternity Gang Rape: Sex, Brotherhood, and Privilege on Campus, *anthropologist Peggy Reeves Sanday records her conversation with a young man named Sean, who recounts how he took great satisfaction in his sense of belonging as he settled into fraternity life. But he also acknowledges how his opinions and actions were dictated by the frat-house culture of misogyny and crude sexual humor.*

Sean joined a fraternity during the second semester of his freshman year. He joined to alleviate the anxiety he felt in the college environment. Coupled with general anxiety about his ability to achieve social and academic success in the new environment was his rebellious attitude toward all authority figures. Joining a fraternity provided a ready solution to both problems. The fraternity provided him with a predetermined role.

Probably because of his experiences with hazing as a boy, when Sean entered college, fraternities seemed like the natural way to deal with anxiety. For Sean and his buddies, most of whom arrived at school bewildered, out of touch with their feelings, and carrying patterns of unresolved emotional problems with their parents and females, the role of "rowdy, inconsiderate and misogynist frat brother" seemed compelling and meaningful. Like Richard Ford, who wrote in *Esquire* (June 1986) about his experience as a brother, Sean thinks of him-

Sean, as told to Peggy Reeves Sanday, in "The Initiation Ritual: A Model for Life," *Fraternity Gang Rape: Sex, Brotherhood, and Privilege on Campus*, 2nd ed., New York: New York University Press, 2007, pp. 149–153.

self as "a go-along guy, who wanted friends. A guy with feelings he couldn't understand." For Sean and boys like him,
"conformity was a godsend."

Sean did not place much value on his own individuality.
He was not assertive, nor did he shape situations or relationships. By his own account, he was "the kind of boy who was
willing to mold and deform myself to fit into something that
was already out there." He was uncertain about his own worth
and his emotional strength. He was looking for situations
where he could "just sort of fit in without making too much
fuss, without having people look at [him] too hard."

> The fraternity seemed to offer just that. They were easygoing
> guys. They joked around a lot, but they were always open
> and friendly, and it seemed that I was accepted without
> question from the very start. A ready-made group of guys
> who were actively trying to get me to join! It made me very
> happy to play hard-to-get for a change.

The Fraternity as Family

Sean recognized that fraternity life also offered a "new family"
to compensate for the loss he felt at leaving his own family.
Although it is a "transitional family," he knew that it would always provide him with a haven in which he could cope with
anxiety and work out his sense of adolescent rebellion.

> When I left home I was both glad and scared to be indepen-
> dent of my parents. I felt sick and tired of their control over
> and constant involvement in my life, but I had never known
> any other way. Although I was noisily proclaiming and cel-
> ebrating my new life as a free agent, I needed a family sub-
> stitute, a tight social situation where I could count on emo-
> tional support. The fraternity provided me that support.
> Since I wasn't very aware of my emotional needs, I didn't go
> on a conscious search for a healthy support group. Instead, I
> thought I just needed a "cool place to hang out" and a regu-
> lar group of friends. Since I and my friends were dealing

with heavy sexual and academic tensions at the same time, it seemed natural to find a noisy group of guys where we could laugh and forget about all these complications of life. In the fraternity, we could deal with many of these problems, or at least escape from them: we could laugh off the expectations we felt from our parents and from society in general to be responsible, mature people. Together, we could deal with sexual and social frustration. When we were together, we could laugh at all the things that made us feel alone and powerless. As a group we could deal aggressively with the issues, and sometimes the people, that made us feel insecure inside. Of course, the way we dealt with our insecurities was not exactly calculated to make anyone else feel better. Thus, while we felt like we were just having some laughs, we were thumbing our noses at (or giving the finger to) social responsibility and parental values. Thinking back now, I realize that our responses to anxiety about the blacks around here were too racist and our responses to sexual frustration and lack of friendship with campus women were too sexist. At the time, we felt like we were just responding to a new environment that seemed hostile and humorless.

Most young men are not able to articulate their reasons for joining a fraternity with the same degree of insight. Another, less reflective brother, explained his motivation for joining a fraternity in terms of the "mystical tendency" for men to form bonds with other men. This young man was attracted by the "feeling of love" he had for the brothers and by the "love" they displayed for one another. In a less idealistic, more pragmatic vein, he also pointed out that a strong incentive was the desire to be one of the select few whose residence in a fraternity placed him at the hub of social life. He relished the sensational central location of the house he chose to join. The house was located in the middle of campus on Fraternity Row, and the prospect of living and dining at this house with the future brothers of his pledge class was a major incentive for joining that house.

The Desire for Status and Identity

Clearly the sense of self-esteem that comes from being one of the chosen few is an important incentive for joining a fraternity. In psychological terms the "mystic tendency" can be understood as the exhilaration of moving from adolescent dependency to the first stage of male dominance and control. The attraction of fraternal bonding is that it confers a status identity on adolescent males who cannot stand on their own. The depth of the emotional bond men feel for their fraternity is explained by the degree to which this bond helps to compensate feelings of inferiority and powerlessness in a society that privileges male bonding. Fraternity brothers do not become friends or teammates or colleagues; they become *brothers*. As Sean explains,

> *Brother* is not an empty term. In my house, brothers travel thousands of miles every year to get together and to help initiate the new members, and commitments to the brotherhood clearly rank in their lives with family and professional commitments.

Brotherhood helped to reassure Sean about his sexual prowess, a continual source of personal worry and sense of inferiority. Sexual joking among the brothers relieved his anxiety and gave him a sense of mastery. Sexual joking, he explains, made the brothers feel good together.

> Any sexual experience was shared with the group. A brother would jokingly thank the rest of us for "helping" him to get laid, either by recruiting a woman for him or by putting on a good party. His success was our success and we would joke about sharing the conquest directly. "Well, now that you've loosened her up for the rest of us . . . ," and we'd all laugh. The humorous references to group sex were always well received. Since some of us were marching band members, the favorite road-trip song, "Gang Bang," was heard regularly. We also liked to share ridiculously exaggerated sexual boasting, such as our mythical "Sixteen Kilometer Flesh-Weapon,"

and double-entendre plays on sexual performance. Example: "How was the exam this morning? *Much too long!* Yeah, that's what *she* said!" Even when this got embarrassingly out of hand (such as when we sent party invitations to alumni, promising to supply imported women "with big breasts and small brains"), it was always fun to laugh over this stuff together. By including me in this perpetual, hysterical banter and sharing laughter with me, they showed their affection for me. I felt happy, confident, and loved. This really helped my feelings of loneliness and my fear of being sexually unappealing. We managed to give ourselves a satisfying substitute for sexual relations. We acted out all of the sexual tensions between us as brothers on a verbal level. *Women, women* everywhere, feminists, homosexuality, etc., all provided the material for the jokes.

After a few months of interacting with the brothers of his fraternity house, Sean found that it became difficult to have a good time with other friends, especially with women, because the special secret understanding was missing and he did not feel comfortable conducting a relationship on any other basis than the one he became accustomed to in the house. By choosing to interact mainly with his brothers, Sean realized that he gave up the possibility of gaining adult autonomy and developing his unique individuality. Instead, he was increasingly molded to the frat-house personality type. Although he chose the fraternity as a stand-in family, in fact the frat-house culture taught him to reject the tenderness and compassion he had learned at home.

Viewing Women as Objects
of Conquest

Michael A. Messner

A professor of sociology and gender studies and author of several books, Michael A. Messner speaks on sex equity and violence in sports to students, academics, educators, and coaches' associations. In this essay, he writes about his experiences as a college basketball player and how he was pressured into trying to entice his girlfriend into having sex with him; in his words to "treat my girlfriend more as an object of conquest than as a person with feelings of her own." As a result, he began to understand how peer groups may persuade members to engage in sexual activity, leading to date rape.

In gang rape, men use female bodies to bond with each other. Anthropologist Peggy Sanday and others who have studied gang rape are careful to argue that, from the point of view of the woman, the rape is not a sexual experience but a violent, degrading, and painful assault. For the perpetrators, however, gang rape certainly is a sexual experience—but it is not about sex with a woman; rather, the males in the group use the violated woman's body as an object through which to have vicarious sex with each other. Underlying gang rape is male anxiety about status in a hierarchy of power, expressed through denigration of women and erotic bonding among men, and rooted in the misogynist joking culture of athletic teams.

Most heterosexual boys and young men go through a period of insecurity and even discomfort in learning to establish

Michael A. Messner, "The Triad of Violence in Men's Sports," *Transforming a Rape Culture*, edited by Emilie Buchwald, Pamela R. Fletcher, and Martha Roth, Minneapolis, MN: Milkweed Editions, 2005, pp. 23–46. Copyright © 2005, Editors' Introduction, Selection, and Arrangement by Emilie Buchwald, Pamela R. Fletcher, and Martha Roth. All rights reserved. Reproduced by permission.

sexual relations with girls and women. Men who were former athletes told me that in high school, and even in college, talking with girls and women made them feel anxious and inadequate. These young men dealt with their feelings of lameness with young women primarily by listening to and watching their male peers deliver a rap to women. This peer pedagogy of heterosexual relations taught them to put on a performance for girls that seemed to work. The success of this learned heterosexual come-on allowed a young man to mask, even overcome, his sense of insecurity and lameness in his own eyes and, just as important, in the eyes of his male teammates. It also deepened his erotic bond with other members of his male peer group by collectively constructing women as objects of conquest.

As a freshman in college, I was a marginal member of my community college basketball team. After having been a reasonably good high school player, I found myself thirteenth on a thirteen-player team. Moreover, off the court I could not hold my own in the competitive sexual banter. Early in the season, on a road trip, the guys lounged around in a motel room, talking and joking about sex. Drew, our starting center and one of the highest-status guys on the team, noticed that Rob (another marginal player) and I had not been contributing anything to the raucous chronicling of sexual exploits. "Hey, Robby T., hey Mess," Drew asked, "you guys ever had a piece of ass?"

A virgin with little to brag about, I tensed up. Kess, another reserve player, had recently been labeled the team fag after he refused to jump into the middle of a brawl with another team. I wanted to avoid becoming such a target of joking put-downs, so I employed what I thought was a subtle strategy. "Naw," I replied, but with diverted eyes and a knowing smile I hoped would suggest I was simply too cool to brag about sex with my girlfriend, a high school girl. Rob followed the same strategy. Drew, missing the subtleties, clobbered us:

"Wow! We got two virgins on this team! We can't have that! Mess, Robby T., we gotta get you laid, and soon! We can't go having any virgins on the team. Havin' Kess is bad enough!"

The Pressure Increases

A couple of weeks later, Drew invited us to a party. Robby T. and I showed up together, with our six-packs of beer. Soon Drew announced to Rob and me, loudly, "Hey, you two virgins ain't gonna be virgins after tonight, eh?" Not knowing what he was talking about, we just agreed and laughed, "Sure, Drew. We're trying to figure out who we're going to lay tonight." Drew replied, "Man, you don't have to worry about that, because me and the guys have taken care of it. We got a lady comin' over here in a couple of hours. She's real special, and since you guys are the only two virgins on the team, you get to go first." As I felt my palms get sweaty, I knew I was supposed to act grateful. "Wow, Drew. Like, is she some kind of prostitute or something?"

Drew smiled. "You could say that. She's kind of a friend of mine, you know?" He laughed loud and hard, and so did we. I took some long pulls on my beer, drained it, and opened another one, I whispered to Robby T., "Let's get the hell out of here," and we escaped out the back door.

Rob and I never did find out whether Drew was serious about his plan to get us laid, or if the guys were just pulling a joke on the two lower-status guys on the team. We felt a bit ashamed, and we knew that leaving the party did nothing to enhance our status, so we decided that the way to handle the guys when we next saw them was to lie: We were now laying our girlfriends and just couldn't do it with someone else because we were faithful. That's how we escaped being put in the fag bag with Kess. We were accepted now; we had learned how to bullshit with the best of them.

After this embarrassing incident, I began to step up the pressure on my girlfriend to put out. Like many young men, I wanted to have sex. But the urgency of my desire was not driven simply by my attraction to my girlfriend. I desperately wanted access to the sexual experience that would put me on a par with the guys on the team. Fortunately, my girlfriend had a mind of her own and asserted her own timetable for what we would do and when we would do it. However, I can see in retrospect how my experiences with my teammates evoked fear, embarrassment, and frustration over my virgin status, and this in turn encouraged a tendency to treat my girlfriend more as an object of conquest than as a person with feelings of her own. This experience eventually helped me to understand how athletic male peer groups' voyeuring—forming bonds by watching each other have sex or listening to each other talk about sex—works. It doesn't always lead to gang rape; it can also feed a more private dynamic of date and acquaintance rape, even among young men who are marginal in their athletic peer group.

A Psychiatrist Speaks Out About His Views on Rape

Slava Ellis

Psychiatrist Slava Ellis candidly states his opinions on the male and female sides of sexual assault in this interview with antirape activist Timothy Beneke. Ellis views the belief that men can be pushed easily over the edge sexually as a form of intimidation of women. He feels men must battle against the culture that insists that they be competitive and suppress emotion, which leads to the objectification of women. On the other hand, he asserts that women often feel that they have sexual power over men, don't understand this power very well, but hesitate to give it up by demanding less provocative advertising, movies, and so forth. In addition, he details other aspects of the culture of rape in American society.

Some of [French author Marquis] de Sade's writings were sexually exciting to me when I was about eighteen. What was exciting to me was de Sade's ability to create a whole other world of sexual possibilities. He did all these weird, awful things to women with no qualms, no guilt. In *Justine* I remember thinking "I hope something nice happens to her," but it was one catastrophe after another. What's interesting about the fantasies I recall is that the woman is basically faceless. The power isn't over another creature but over another body. It relates to the whole omnipotent male attitude, the Pygmalion myth: the idea that I'll f--- her and she'll finally realize what life is all about. . . .

Previously, it wasn't necessary for men to relate to women intimately as people different from themselves, but now it is.

It's hard to make a distinction between expressing your power and manipulation. There's an extreme form of manipulation where you're clearly manipulating someone, but there's a gray area that needs to encompass your understanding of the person you're relating to. The same behavior might be asserting your power to another man and manipulation to a woman. So a woman might feel manipulated when you didn't want or intend to manipulate.

Have you ever felt sympathetic to the common myths about rape, i.e., that women can't be raped, or that women who claimed to have been raped were really consenting?

I've never believed those myths. I felt sympathetic to them after encountering a fair number of men who felt that way, sympathetic in the sense that I could feel their frustration and denial and chaos, which comes from feeling that they've *had enough*, enough erotic stimulation. You could call it feeling "prick teased," which to a considerable degree is how men grow up. It's not often talked about. The exceptions in my adolescence tended to be either wimpy secluded scholar types who didn't seem to feel their sexuality much, or people who ran in the fast crowd who were getting sex.

My own experience of all this sexual stimulation was on the one hand feeling impotent, and on the other yearning for sexual experience and not knowing how to find it or whether I would be able to run the social risks involved. The necessity of being aggressively and suavely seductive took me five years to learn, and was something I resented because it really didn't get me what I wanted, which was tenderness and love and acceptance. Instead it intensified the degree to which I objectified women. My fantasy was that if you're forceful at just the right time, she'll give in and you'll get laid—the Hollywood paradigm. My experience was that if I were forceful, but not physical, I usually was able to seduce the woman, but if I became at all physical, which happened once or twice when my own urges got out of hand, the woman backed off really quickly, which frightened me. . . .

The issue to me is that men are imprinted much like ducks on certain forms, textures, skins, whatever sexual stimulation they grew up with. And for centuries the only power women have had is as sexual stimulation for men. Sexual stimuli trigger a whole sequence of emotions and behavior that are very hard to stop. And many women don't take responsibility for it because it's the only power they've had. It was communicated to them in a very ambivalent and charged way by their mothers and the culture that you don't really talk about your sexual power, but you use it. Women are in a bind: if they don't behave like sex objects they get punished for it, and if they do they dehumanize themselves. The women I know who are successful know how to say no in very clear definite ways in addition to being very proud of how they look.

If men weren't so overstimulated sexually, they'd find it much easier to relate to women as people. I'd like to see lawyers take on sexist advertising, which reinforces the idea that women are willing and ready.

The men I've known who've felt sympathetic to rapists feel as if a boil's ready to burst. Emotions and wants surge about inside that they can't articulate. Most men never learn to express what's inside them. In these men, the frustration stems from a thwarted need to be held and touched. And not getting what they want, their only recourse, given that all of America says you have to get laid to be a man, is to wind up feeling that the only way to treat a woman is to rape her.

The men I'm talking about would agree that taking another person's sexuality is not very different from taking their life. But they also feel that rape can be justified. The attitude is: "I'll kill anybody who raped my wife, but that broad walking down the street who's wiggling her ass too much deserves to be raped": the only way to quiet what's been stirred up is to rape her. . . .

The nearest analogue to rape for women that I'm aware of is the pre-Christian Greek Dionysian festivals which happened twice yearly in which women left their husbands and families and ran amok in the streets. Young goats were especially prized and women tore them apart with their hands and teeth, and in some festivals there are historical accounts of men being torn apart. It was a frenzy devoted to expressing the kind of frustration women must have felt at being treated as chattel. It comes out of the same kind of impotence men feel currently.

Male Dominance

What do men have to gain by allowing rape to flourish?

What they have to gain is easy intimidation of their wives or the women they're with, keeping women "in their place," keeping them afraid to go out. Men know that they wouldn't mind walking out in the street and if they're with a woman there's not going to be any problem and it's tempting for them to even maybe giggle a bit about women being frightened, when all women have to do is carry a gun or go to karate class. But it's clearly not that simple. It's like being a hypocritical bully. . . .

Physical intimidation can be subtly implied. The expectation that a man can be driven crazy or berserk sexually is common. "Of course I have my civilized decency, but if you push me any further I'm going to go nuts." And that's physical intimidation. The male attitude is "I'm really a bully but not taking responsibility for it. I refuse to take responsibility for it beyond this point. If I smell your vaginal secretions, I will go crazy."

What men have to gain by ending rape is a little more long term, because men will be forced to find other ways of maintaining power, their own individual power, rather than their power en masse as men. Men need to confront their blindness. It's a negative incentive in the sense that you have to experience pain in order to grow. You have to experience your own powerlessness, your feminine side, your intolerance, your arrogance, and the deprivation you had to suffer by objectifying women. There's an initial ego loss involved in admitting these things. It's a first step.

Once that's out of the way you have the further pain of experiencing what you repressed and learning to show your feelings and take risks in the midst of a lot of fear. The incentive for going through this is being freer inside, having more control over your destiny and a wider and more intense gamut of emotions. And if you can feel your emotions better you're more likely to have a better orgasm, and more of a true sense of what you want.

There's no indication that many men are willing to go through these processes. It's going to take generations for men to change. Capitalism, Madison Avenue [the advertising industry], and most jobs create fierce competition and require objectification.

The Female Perspective

What has your experience in therapy been with women who've been raped?

Women invariably feel a great deal of chaos and rage and guilt after being raped. I try to focus on helping the woman express her outrage clearly.

Maybe half of the rape victims I've treated have been able to feel their rage and their powerlessness about being raped only after they stopped feeling guilty about the sexual sensations they experienced during the rape. For some women, if they feel anything sexual at all, it retroactively condemns them. Women I've spoken with felt condemned and betrayed by their bodies because they had sexual sensations when they were raped. It is understandable that a woman might experience sexual sensation, and in no way implies that she's masochistic or encouraged it. A common formulation is that if a woman experiences sexual sensations when raped, she either wanted it or she enjoys being punished.

What happens physiologically, in rape, is that because of the fear involved, there's a significant disconnection between the higher cortical centers and what's happening in the rest of your body, so that any mechanical stimulation in the vagina causes primitive centers in your spinal cord to respond, and they send information back through the spinal cord so you feel you're not completely anesthetized, but you don't have any control over the physiological events occurring in your vagina. So, although you don't have any control, you feel responsible, which is a crazy situation to be in.

The rape victim is in a terrible dilemma. She can resist physically and create spasms in the walls of the pelvis and risk physical harm, or she can relax physically and run the risk of experiencing sexual sensations and scarring herself psychically. I'd advise women to relax and experience whatever sexual sensations might arise. The point is that this isn't all you experience. The dominant experience is some massive kind of alienation and fear, a very minor aspect of which might be the sexual sensations, but a woman recalling those sexual sensations will be in a lot of pain in this culture. Either way she tries to deal with the rapist she's bound to get hurt, which is the nature of the crime. . . .

Women quite reasonably don't want to address the subject of sexual sensation in rape victims because many men will try to exploit it, specifically by saying, "Ha, ha, you wanted it all along."

It might be easier to address the issue if the sexual sensations rape victims feel is seen not as giving aid to the enemy, but rather in terms of an understandable physiological response, thereby realizing that women are *not* responsible for whatever sexual sensations arise, and in fact they have been conditioned by men to feel responsible for something they *can't* be responsible for, which is one of the reasons rape flourishes. Women's not admitting the bind men put them in by raping them makes it all that easier for men to rape them. It may keep rape victims from reporting to the police or talking about it to people they feel close to. . . .

There are also a lot of women who don't get caught in this bind and they're the ones who are able to talk more freely about what in fact happened to them, and feel just outraged rather than chaotic about having had sexual sensations. That should be the main object of work on rape: to help women feel their outrage rather than feeling responsible and chaotic.

The subject should be opened up and men should learn to talk about it. From my own experience, men are very frightened of talking about rape. . . .

I have never spoken to male psychiatrists about their ideas, fantasies, or feelings about rape, and I spent three years in psychiatric residency in a good hospital in Boston in the early seventies. Men are afraid to address their feelings and fantasies about rape, afraid they'll uncover something in themselves, because they want to deny the possibility of having rape feelings. The classic explanation is that if you're really terrified to talk about something like this, the eventual analysis is that you also want it very much, so it's possible men are afraid to talk about rape because it turns them on, but I'm only speculating.

How Rape Is Promoted in Culture

How does Hollywood support rape?

There's the classic movie scene in which the hero kisses the heroine against her will, and a struggle ensues, and he's overwhelming her and there's always one moment which is underscored, in which her resistance and struggle turn to moaning and heavy breathing and surrender.

The message for women is: pleasure will make you powerless. As soon as you start having sexual sensations, you will be powerless.

The message for men is: you can inflict pleasure on a woman against her will. This message appeals enormously to frustrated men.

What are the psychodynamics of rapists?

I think rapists probably destroy their feminine sides, what [Swiss psychiatrist Carl] Jung called the anima. The destruction of the man's anima comes in all the different, probably multifarious, steps you need to go through in objectifying the woman to the point of being able to rape her. The man denies his feminine side so that he is unable to identify with the woman. The woman becomes the other, the unrecognizable, the one that needs to be vanquished, the prize that will assuage your own pain. I think rape proceeds initially from pain and then rage, to action. In order to prevent rape, you need to feel your sadness but you can't feel your sadness because that'll make you feel less of a man. In fact, if you feel the sadness you feel refreshed and much better able to deal with what the issues are afterward. So there's a flagrant lie going on. What is the function of that lie? When I've lied to myself about my sadness, it was to keep me from feeling vulnerable, as if it would turn me into a woman with all the negative connotations of being weak, being used, being unable to move. The social pressures against a man showing his sadness are real.

The very act of lying about your sadness and having to repress it accentuates your rage. If you feel your sadness and go through it you can still feel indignant and mad at somebody who hurt you, but you won't want to kill them or rape them. Rapists are unable to feel sadness in a way that relieves them. Anything feminine in themselves is very threatening. You would have to be out of touch with the feminine self to develop that degree of distance and objectification in order to rape. Rapists need to overcome the feminine and subjugate it and make sure that it stays down, and the final blow is the rape itself. . . .

Is there any truth to the notion that a man can be provoked by a woman's appearance and lose control of himself?

Well, men obviously have a choice on the basis of their feelings. You can feel whatever you want, but if you hurt someone because of it that's completely different.

I really don't think it's possible that the way a woman acts or dresses could in fact mechanistically elicit a complex sequence of behavioral events. It's impossible. It might be more difficult for some men to control themselves if the basal level of certain brain chemicals is different, but that's still speculation and hasn't been shown.

If you're opposed to sexism in advertising are you also opposed to pornography?

The double side of the dilemma is that women grow up at least unconsciously realizing that the way they look gives them a tremendous amount of power. To give up sexism in advertising women have to confront giving up that power as a manipulation and I don't think women are at all willing to do that today. The lesbian contingent certainly is, and maybe one in ten nonlesbians would.

Most women are unwilling to condemn sexist advertising because they don't want to confront the whole issue of how powerful their sexuality can be. If they confront that then they're going to be terrified. A large part of the terror of rape is not knowing your own power.

Nice Boys Can Do Bad Things

Judith V. Becker

Now a professor of psychology and psychiatry, Judith Becker was studying for her doctorate when she was asked to help on a pioneering study of sexual deviance and adult sex offenders. Twenty years later, she has earned an international reputation as an expert for her work with juvenile sex offenders. She explains what she has learned about the traits often seen in juveniles who will go on to engage in sexual assault, what she calls "a deviant sexual-interest pattern." She stresses that this behavior is not limited to minority teens from troubled backgrounds and that there are definite cultural factors that contribute to violent sexual behavior.

Back when my supervisor and I worked with adult sex offenders, we learned that 60 percent had started committing the crimes when they were juveniles. And they had committed hundreds if not thousands of sexual crimes during their lifetime. We also learned that they can have what we call a deviant sexual-interest pattern. I'll explain that.

Years ago, the belief was that peeping toms were just peeping toms. We didn't have to worry they'd do anything else. Exhibitionists? They were just shy. Showing us their penis was their way of asking for a date.

Well, those beliefs were wrong. For example, half of these "shy" exhibitionists had fantasies about or had engaged in sexual acts with children. About 20 percent of them had fantasies about or had raped adults.

We also learned to be concerned about young boys . . . [who]:

- Make obscene phone calls

- Engage in voyeuristic (peeping tom) behavior

- Show their penis to somebody

- Mistreat animals

- Dress up in women's clothing

- Stalk and humiliate their classmates

- Rehearse assaults

We even had examples of boys acting out assaults with their teddy bears. Often people write it off as "boys being boys," and in some cases, it may be. In other cases, however, this is the start. It leads to more serious sexual crimes.

Advice for Young Males

Now I'm talking more directly to the male readers. Think of the behaviors I mentioned this way. Some of you kids take a drink or smoke a joint at ages eight, nine, or ten. Not all of you become alcoholics or go on to mainline drugs. But a certain percentage of you will, and you should be concerned if you think you might be part of that percentage.

Thoughts—in this case, your sexual thoughts—are much harder to uncover. If you have thoughts involving sex with relatives—if you think about doing sexual things with a brother, sister, mother, whoever—you need to be concerned. If you have thoughts about *forcing* sex on someone, you need to be concerned. If you like seeing people being hurt, injured, or shamed, you need to be concerned about that, too.

Most importantly, you should never masturbate to any of those thoughts. The masturbation reinforces the behavior.

What people think about sexually and what they reinforce through masturbation can be a rehearsal for the actual deviant behavior.

If you behave this way or have these kinds of sexual thoughts, you're not a bad person. It just means you need help. Find a trusted adult to put you in contact with programs that deal with these problems.

Thoughts on Curiosity

You kids *are* curious about sex. It's normal to feel aroused by or attracted to people. Sex can be healthy behavior when engaged in responsibly and at an age when you are aware of the risks and the benefits.

But normal sexual curiosity and behavior involves two people of the same age, both agreeing to do something. There's no threat. No bribe.

Curiosity is not a fifteen-year-old and a five-year-old. Curiosity is not two seven-year-olds where one is holding a stick and saying, "Show me your vagina or I'll hit you." Curiosity is not two people of the same age, one with an IQ of 120 and the other with an IQ of 50.

I'm a researcher. While I don't have the data to support it, my sense is there's an increase in deviant sexual behavior among teenagers. One reason I think we're in such a mess now is that adults are not open to your curiosity about sex. Adults don't want to talk about it.

On the nightly news, though, there are routine reports about sexual assault. Even little kids watching TV can hear about things like gang rape. Television allows you to learn about sexual misuse when you haven't yet learned about healthy sexuality.

A Violent Nation

We're a violent society that objectifies women. Consequently, we have a higher rate of rape than other countries. And the states within our nation with the highest rates have widespread approval of what we might call legitimate violence—the death penalty, few restrictions on carrying guns, and residents who are into violent contact sports, such as football.

On the other hand, in the Scandinavian countries, for example, there are laws against the death penalty, carrying guns, and so on, as well as much more openness about sexuality. As a result, the rape rates are much lower. In our country, we think if adults talk to kids about sex, you're going to go out and be sexual. There are no data, however, to support that.

More and more of you are growing up in families where you see parents bring multiple partners into the home. You're not being parented. You're being left alone to abuse your peers, and you are being placed in the role of baby-sitter, where you can initiate younger kids into sex. In addition, many of you are being abused by a parent, a sibling, or a next-door neighbor.

We must be concerned about the abused becoming the abuser. We know that sexually abused boys are at greater risk of becoming abusers themselves. In fact, 40 percent of sex offenders have been sexually abused. Sixty percent were physically abused.

When I say "sexually abused," I've heard of every type of act imaginable: sexual intercourse, masturbating, being masturbated, oral sex, foreign objects being inserted into the anus, fondling, and so on.

Previous Abuse

Initially when we started to work with juvenile sex offenders, we asked them, "Have you ever been sexually abused?" We realized, however, it's difficult to admit that. So we began to say, "We'd like you to tell us about every person with whom you've had a sexual experience."

And then we ask, "How old were you?" "How old was the other person?" "Was this person a relative?" "Was this other person male or female?" With that last question, we found that boys are less likely to disclose sexual contact they've had with a woman. Yet when we say, "Did you initiate the behavior?" the answer is no.

"Do you define that as sexual abuse?" we ask them.

"No."

"Why not?"

"Well, boys are supposed to feel lucky if a woman has sex with them."

"If a man did that to you, would it be sexual abuse?" we ask.

"Yes."

Some sexually abused boys act it out either sexually against other people or their overall aggressive behavior may increase. But not all do that. They develop empathy because they have been the victim. They never do anything like that to other people.

We also know that sexually abused girls internalize their pain. They turn it in against themselves. In other words, girls usually develop anxiety disorders. They may get depressed. If they act it out, they may become sexually promiscuous.

Rapists Are a Mixed Group

Rapists are a mixed group. Their motivation varies. However, some individuals—we call them antisocial—do not care about other people's feelings. They have no sense of right and wrong. These people rob, maim, and rape. They commit what are known as crimes of opportunity.

Say a man breaks into an apartment to take the money, the TV, and the VCR. Unknown to him, a woman's sleeping in the next room. He sees her and thinks, "As long as I'm here, I might as well rape her." So he does.

Some individuals are only turned on by violent sex. They may have a girlfriend, they may be married. But when the person agrees to sex, it's not erotic—not sexy—to them.

Others aren't severely mentally ill, but they are intellectually limited. They may be twenty-year-olds but have the mental age of a ten-year-old. Because they are more comfortable around ten-year-olds, maybe they sexualize the relationship.

Still others are severely mentally ill or have something wrong with part of their brain. They have trouble controlling their thinking and their general behavior. They see someone, feel an attraction, and act on that feeling by forcing sex on that person.

Date Rape

Teenagers are more likely to run into these kinds of situations: under the influence of alcohol or drugs—which we know affects our ability to control our behavior—you do things you wouldn't normally do, including rape.

That's not an excuse for the behavior. It's what happens and it means you should stay away from those things.

When males get together, some feel a way of asserting or proving their masculinity is by showing how macho they are. A way to do that is by having sex—all of them raping one girl.

The fact is that rape is not an expression of masculinity. It's an expression of cowardice. Anyone sure of himself doesn't have to engage in a cowardly act by forcing sex on another person—particularly when the odds are so much in the gang's favor.

Still other individuals prefer to have sex with a peer and prefer to have consensual sex—sex that both people agree to. But when that person isn't available, or that person says no, then they force sex on either that person or another person. A lot of date rapes fall into this category.

Boys need to know that when a girl says no, you respect that no. And girls need to know that if you mean no, you should say no. If you mean yes, you should say yes. However, if you say yes to some things but no to other things, you have to be clear.

Sexual behavior starts with looking at someone you find attractive. The next step is wanting that person to notice you. Maybe after that, you go out. You want to touch that person.

But you need the person's permission. So maybe you kiss, but again you need the other person's permission to kiss.

After that, maybe you want to do some upper-body touching. Still, though, you need the other person's permission. Next might be that you want some genital touching. Once again you need permission.

The person can give permission anywhere along the line. But at a critical point, permission might not be granted for whatever reason—sexually transmitted diseases, fear of pregnancy, the girl wants to wait until she is an adult in a committed relationship.

Boys need to be prepared to stop anywhere in that process. Girls have to be prepared to say no and to mean it. When a girl says, "No, no, no . . . well, okay," the boy is confused. And I am in no way holding girls responsible for being assaulted or the victims of date rape.

Working with the Perpetrator

Men rape because it makes them feel powerful. They want to humiliate the other person. Most importantly, they are aroused by the behavior. They get erections. Sometimes, but not always, they ejaculate.

Some people say there's nothing sexual about rape; that rape is purely violence. That's not true. It's sex and violence. At sexual behavior clinics, we treat adolescents between the ages of thirteen and eighteen who have misused their sexuality.

Lots of people see them as scum and say, "We should execute them." Others say, "No, we should castrate them." Studies have been done on castrating individuals. First of all, we can remove a person's testicles and they still get erections. Remove the penis, too? A person doesn't need a penis to molest someone. He still has his hands, his mouth, foreign objects. So that's not going to solve the problem.

Lock up the person? Yes, that would stop them from committing sexual crimes for as long as they're in jail. But most people eventually get out, and when they do they start all over again. Jail is not the solution.

Yesterday I was on TV. People wanted to know how nice kids could rape. I said, "Unfortunately, nice boys can do bad things." People don't buy that. They think if you do something bad, you're a bad person. The fact is there are nice people who do horrible things. But you don't throw away the person. You try to change the behavior. That's where clinics come in.

Clinics vary, but programs often offer outpatient treatment free of charge. Youngsters are evaluated so we can see what their needs and strengths are. Initially, the therapy is individual and then they are moved into groups. Because most kids deny or minimize what they did, one goal is to help them accept full responsibility.

In the process we want to know how they gave themselves permission to do what they did. How did they justify the behavior? Then we challenge that and try to give them other ways of looking at situations and at their actions.

We also look at risky situations to them, the early warning signs to their behavior. We teach them how to avoid those situations. We teach them the effects of their behavior on their victims and how this can continue for the rest of the victims' lives.

Then we help them develop the skills to maintain good relationships with their peers. Because we're taking something away, we must make sure they know how to have future relationships that are good ones.

But we're like an oasis. They come here and we try to undo a lot of what society has done. When the boys leave, we pray to God that they will maintain what they've learned. The truth? They won't find a whole lot of reinforcement out there.

SOCIAL ISSUES
FIRSTHAND

CHAPTER 2

Surviving Date and Acquaintance Rape

A Story of Gang Rape

"Amy"

This particular assault, a gang rape, was carried out at a fraternity party. The author of the book from which this story was taken, anthropologist Peggy Reeves Sanday, has named the fraternity "RST house," has given the young woman a fictitious name (Amy), and has withheld the name of the university to protect the victim. Amy very honestly describes the events surrounding her rape. As with a good number of sexual assault occurrences, alcohol consumption and subsequent impaired judgment played a significant part. She explains that she was flattered by the attention she had received previously from the fraternity men and loved to feel that she was attractive. Thinking she was in control of her sexual encounters, Amy learned that, sadly, she was not.

Early one morning, after a late night party at the RST house at the beginning of my junior year, I was raped by I don't know how many guys. I had been going to RST parties since I was a freshman, even though I was warned on the first day of orientation never to go to the house alone.

The RST guys were known to be a rowdy crew, heavy drinkers and "partyers." I started going there in October of my freshman year and went about three times a week during that year. From the first time I went, the brothers were kind of friendly. At least they noticed me. At other fraternities I was treated as a complete nonentity.

The RST brothers did a lot of weird things. They had this doll they called "Troll." It was a plastic blowup doll, about life size. The guys would carry it around. I never really under-

"Amy," in "Other Victims, Other Campuses," *Fraternity Gang Rape: Sex, Brotherhood, and Privilege on Campus*, by Peggy Reeves Sanday, 2nd ed., New York: New York University Press, 2007, pp. 110–117. Copyright © 2007 by New York University. All rights reserved. Reproduced by permission.

stood the significance of this doll. It seemed as if it represented the girls the brothers picked up, because the doll was always mentioned in connection with a brother who had managed to get laid. The brothers referred to women at the parties as trolls, particularly women they thought less of. If a brother did not manage to pick up a woman at a party, the other brothers would make jokes about him spending the night with this doll, Troll-Ann. It seemed as if the doll got more respect than the women the brothers had sex with.

Girlfriends were treated with more respect. There were different classes of women associated with RST. In addition to the girlfriends, who didn't go much to the parties, there were the little sisters. A prerequisite to being a little sister was sleeping with the brothers. That was just sort of accepted. The little sisters were never treated too well. But, there was a stratum of women even lower than the little sisters, the stratum I belonged to. This class of women, called Trolls, consisted of those who went to the parties and slept with the brothers but did not demand in return the status of girlfriend or little sister. The difference between the Trolls and the little sisters was that during the week the little sisters could drop by the house on a friendly basis and the Trolls could not.

The brothers marked women who came to their parties with something called power dots. They were black, red, yellow, white, and blue colored dots that the brothers would stick to a girl's clothing at parties.

I'm not sure what the dots meant. Someone said that they indicated how good a friend you were to RST. The estimate for how good a friend you were was based on how easy you were to pick up, with white being the most difficult, then yellow, then blue, red, and with black being the easiest. They put blue, sometimes yellow or orange dots on me. I never saw them put black on anyone because that was really pushing it. But they joked about the black dot. They put red on girls who had been there before, girls who were blatantly interested in picking up guys. White was mostly for girls who had never been there before, and who looked really sweet, or who weren't sorority. They weren't interested in sorority women. I think the dots helped to mark women for other men so they would know where to start. For example, if a woman had a white dot, you didn't say really raunchy things to her when you first met her. If she had a red dot you didn't start off by asking her what her major was.

Feeling Powerful

The parties were for sex and drinking. People would sort of go back and forth between the bedrooms and the party. I first started sleeping with somebody about maybe three weeks after I started going to RST. It was very late and I'd been at the party for hours. At that point I don't think there were even any women left at the party. I felt like I could pick and choose among the guys. Being able to do that made me feel kind of powerful. It seemed like the thing to do, like that was what was expected of me, and it was no big deal.

After I had slept with a brother the first time, brothers would approach me fairly directly and say, "Do you want to go to my room with me?" As an incentive they would offer grain punch or pot. If I agreed to go that meant having sex. If I said no, that meant I was saying no to sex. In all, I must have slept with six different RST brothers.

I only slept with Tim on a regular basis. The other guys I slept with because I wasn't feeling real happy and I thought sex would make me feel better. But Tim was somebody I'd sort of staked out earlier on. Someone I liked and thought was kind of cool. I slept with him for the first time after Christmas break of my freshman year.

Tim was kind of weird. There were two occasions when he asked somebody else to join us in a sort of ménage à trois situation. At the time I wasn't comfortable with the situation, but because it was Tim, I felt it was okay. It wasn't that bad, but I wasn't that comfortable with the way I looked nude.

The guys didn't touch each other when we had sex. Usually one of them would just kind of hang out and watch while the other one and I were involved. It was kind of a voyeuristic situation.

The first time it happened it was with a good friend of Tim's who was not very attractive. I got the feeling that Tim was doing him a favor. Sort of like, "you can have her for a while." The other time he had sort of talked to the guy ahead of time. We were sitting around in this other guy's room and we were talking and drinking when Tim started making sexual moves towards me. I was real uncomfortable, because this other man was in the room. Tim said, "How would you feel about him, you know, kind of joining in?"

I was like, "I guess that's okay."

But I'm not real sure what was going on there. That particular guy had a reputation at RST for being one of the easy brothers. He was known for being able to pick up good-looking women with no problem. I don't know why Tim arranged for the three of us to have sex.

Keeping It Casual

The relationship with Tim was real off and on until December of my sophomore year. After that I didn't go there much. I didn't love Tim but I thought he was neat. I prided myself on being the sort who could have a casual relationship. I was also sleeping with other men. Keeping a head count was sort of a point of pride with me. I liked shocking my friends, none of whom were sleeping with anyone. I also wanted to prove to them that I was attractive to men.

It was the same thing in high school. I lost my virginity in order to shock and impress my friends, all of whom were virgins. It was when I was sixteen, the day after my sixteenth birthday. I wanted to get it over with because I thought that once I had lost my virginity I could move on to bigger and better things. Of course, it didn't really work out that way.

My friends thought that what I had done was very adult and kind of sophisticated. It shattered an image I had in high school of being kind of intellectual—a bookwormy type of person. I was really getting tired of that image and I needed to shatter it. I got very involved with a guy who made me pregnant. He was a real loser; he was into dealing drugs, and he had been arrested three or four times by the time he was sixteen or so, but I thought he was neat. His whole family found out I was pregnant before he did. I had told his sister and she spilled it to her mother. They were all shocked. After he found out I still saw him but we didn't go out again.

After that I didn't get involved with anyone for years. I couldn't deal with a romantic relationship because it made me feel really vulnerable and I didn't want to feel that way. So, I guess when I went to college and started going to RST parties I wasn't expecting much from men or from myself. I was willing to please Tim sexually. I didn't get much out of it except a reputation that I felt good about.

Things Begin to Change

I didn't go to RST so much during my sophomore year. But, I was still sleeping on and off with Tim. I was kind of changing my attitudes toward sex. I didn't want to be quite so casual. For me that meant not going to RST so much. In the eight months before I got raped, I probably went about three times. Once I slept with another brother, not Tim. Tim was real relaxed about the situation. When he saw me at a party he would say, "Well, you haven't come to the house much." I would answer, "Well, I've been sort of busy."

During the summer after my sophomore year, I lived in a fraternity, just half a block away from RST. I went to RST parties twice during the summer. They were different than the parties during the year. There were all kinds of people there, not just brothers. But the parties still had this general RST sort of feel in the air, like you didn't know what was going to happen next.

The morning I was raped, I had started drinking at a party we had at our apartment earlier in the evening. It was just after the first day of classes. One of my friends from another university was up. I went to the RST party with this girl. She was really high on drugs. I was really drunk. Earlier in the evening I had blacked out for an hour at about nine-thirty or ten and the next thing I remembered was that we were eating a sandwich on our way to the fraternity.

When we got to the frat there was a party in session. They had a nasty purple punch that had grain alcohol in it. I started drinking and lost track of my friend. Some brothers came downstairs where I was and invited me upstairs to the balcony in front of the house. There were about fifteen to twenty people on the balcony, two or three women and the rest brothers and pledges. My friend had met this guy who was a pledge and she went off with him.

I ran into Tim. He was in high spirits because he had finally graduated. He'd done really well. He was all excited. We chatted and at some point somebody suggested that we eat hoagies in their room. After we had eaten a hoagie, Tim asked if I wanted to go to his room. I agreed, I thought that would be fine.

The Rape Set-Up

We went to his room and talked for a while. We ended up sleeping together. That was kind of okay. He hadn't seen me since about May. Over the summer I'd lost some weight. I was working out every day and I guess I looked really good. Anyway, he kept commenting on how good I looked. His comments made me feel uncomfortable, because he'd never really mentioned how I'd looked before.

After we had sex I had to use the bathroom. Since he didn't have a robe, I wrapped a bath towel around myself. I didn't feel all that naked. I walked out into the hall. There were probably people in the hall, but I don't really remember. He came to the bathroom with me to watch the door because it didn't lock.

When we got to the room there was somebody else in the room. He was lying on the bed and I don't think he had any clothes on at the time. Tim told me to go ahead into the room. I didn't remember seeing the guy before and wanted to know who he was. I was kind of confused. I thought maybe this was another one of those situations where Tim wanted a threesome but he hadn't said anything to me. He hadn't introduced me to this guy, which was kind of weird.

I sat down on the edge of the bed where the guy was lying. The bed was a bunk bed and that was the only place in the room to sit. I wasn't really into standing for any extended period of time. It was beyond my capability. I guess he started kissing me. I was sort of willing. I was sort of passive about it. It didn't really matter.

Then, Tim left and closed the door behind him. I sat up and said, "Where did Tim go?"

And this guy was like, "Don't worry about Tim now."

And I'm like, "I don't understand what's going on."

I'm not even sure what he said. Basically, he said something like, "You'll understand what's going on," or "You'll see."

Next, the door opened and some other guys came in. I think maybe two or three came in at that point. Then, I don't know how, but I went from sitting on the edge of the bed to lying down without the towel wrapped around me. Before, I'd been sitting and wearing the towel on the edge of the bed and then I was lying on the bed without the towel and this guy was on top of me, and there was intercourse going on. Then, the other guys in the room would either come over and one would be like touching me while another was having intercourse or whatever. There was somebody leaning on me most of the time, which made me feel like I was being held down. One person sat on the bed and the other person would sit on my chest with their penis in my mouth or something. It was not like they were saying, "You can't leave," but I felt like that's what they were saying.

At various times, I said, "That hurts, please stop doing it, please leave me alone."

All I heard them saying was, "That doesn't hurt, you like that. You don't want to leave now."

At one point there was some anal penetration, which was really painful. I was crying and somebody held my hand. I said, "This really hurts."

And they said, "Don't worry, it's not with you that long." So I got the impression that somebody knew that I was not enjoying this. That was only the first twenty minutes. It was about three-thirty in the morning.

I knew the time because I went into the room at about three. My girlfriend Molly had gone into Pete's room at a little after three. At the time she went into Pete's room I was still eating hoagies with Tim. It was right after we ate hoagies that I went into Tim's room.

The Next Morning

After the first twenty minutes or so I passed out and didn't wake up until about six in the morning, because I got back into my apartment at six-fifteen. When I woke up there was some guy sitting on my chest with his knees on both sides of my head. I told him to get the hell off me. I'd seen him earlier in the evening, and he said, "What are you doing? I haven't come yet."

I said, "So what, I don't care whether you have. Do you think I have? Get off me."

There was another guy in the room. I was staring at him and looking around the room, trying to figure out what I was doing there, what the guy on top of me was doing, and what the other guy was doing in the room. I wondered why I didn't have any clothes on. These guys left the room and I got dressed and went home.

I felt terrible. I still had my contacts in, which meant that I must have passed out. I always take my contact case with me when I go out at night, because if I sleep with someone I always take my contacts out and put them into the case. I don't think I've ever been so drunk that I didn't take my contacts out if I had the case. When I woke up that morning with them in, my eyes were puffy and swollen, and my face was puffed.

My eyes were puffy from crying also. My lips were bleeding and my jaws were stiff. I couldn't smile. My mouth hurt and my lips felt raw. My anus and vagina also felt sore.

I must have blacked out after Tim left the room. For two hours the guys must have been coming in and out. I knew what happened in the beginning and I knew that when I regained contact with reality, there was still somebody sitting on me trying to force his penis in my mouth. At that point I was able to do something. Earlier, I had been too blacked out to protest or even to have more than a vague awareness of what was happening.

The next morning I knew I had been the victim of a gang bang. At first I thought of it as a gang bang. Sometimes when I was at the house, I had heard the brothers singing a song that went something like, "When I'm older and turning grey, I'll only gang bang once a day."

A pledge told me about a gang bang he had witnessed in his room. It happened while he was asleep on the top bunk in his room during a party. This woman had come in and passed out on the bunk below him. A little later, some brothers just sort of happened into the room. Then a series of them, I don't know how many, more than six, came in and had intercourse with her. They dropped the rubbers on a pile next to the bed. The next morning when she went to get out of bed she stepped in the pile of rubbers.

All the Wrong Reasons

You might ask why I slept with guys at RST knowing that I could get gang banged and knowing that the guys there didn't exactly respect the girls they slept with. I guess I was looking for warmth, some points, a feeling of comfort. Or, maybe just reassurance that I was attractive sexually. Maybe also I felt it gave me some power. I thought I could pick and choose whatever man I was going to sleep with and this gave me a feeling of power to be able to say to some guy, "No, I don't want to sleep with you," or "Yes, I do."

I also liked to court danger. Being warned against going to RST was the incentive to make me go. There was a certain thrill in going someplace that I knew had a bad reputation, where it was hard to say what was going to happen next. I also liked going someplace where my name was known, where I would be recognized when I walked into the room—even if they were kind of jerks. I wasn't particularly good about looking out for myself at the time. I was drinking a lot, sleeping with people I didn't know. I was just not real responsible for myself. I was also hitchhiking lots for fun. I really like the feeling of facing danger.

I also wanted to experience danger in order to learn what it was like so that I could help others. I have always wanted to be a social worker. From a very early age I thought that it was important to experience things in order to learn how to help others. In high school I drank a lot because I felt it was important to be an alcoholic in order to help alcoholics. I also felt that I had to experience problematic relationships in order to effectively help someone else deal with them. The first thought I had when I got my positive pregnancy test was,

"Oh, good, in ten years from now, when I'm a social worker, I'll really know how to deal with this one."

At the time of the RST incident I was drinking once a week. The night of the incident I drank a lot because my friend was up. I really don't know why I drank so much that night. It had been a long time since I had blacked out.

The day after the rape I felt real stupid about being in such a vulnerable position. I was very angry at myself for getting drunk. This made me feel that I was somewhat responsible, but I felt that they were also responsible. And so I went to the IFC [Inter-Fraternity Council] in order to tell them about the incident. The council agreed with my definition of the event as rape and the fraternity was thrown off campus.

Reading News of My Rapist

Maureen Gibbon

Hearing of her rapist years after the assault, Maureen Gibbon records how she felt when she was raped and during the aftermath. She describes how she has come to her present attitude toward the trauma of the past.

Gibbon is the author of a novel and a book of poetry.

One day several years ago, I opened up my hometown newspaper and found a picture of my rapist on the Engagements page.

Maybe I shouldn't have been surprised. I knew he stayed in the area. But it still shocked me to see his photo. He was marrying a younger woman, one with a child, according to the article.

Before the rape, I didn't really know him. He was in his 20's, and he often sat drinking at the bar of the restaurant where I waited on tables when I was 16. One night, rather than ignoring him when he flirted with me, I said yes, I'd go out with him. I willingly got into his truck. But instead of taking me on a date, he drove to the lake outside of town and raped me until my skin tore. I don't mean I was a virgin until that night. I mean that's how violent it was.

When I saw his smiling face in the paper, I found it unbelievable that he had gone on to live what appeared to be a normal life, or that he could have won anyone's heart. But he did. And he was going to be a stepfather. That's what really got me: He was going to live in a house where a young girl would turn 16 one day. I wondered if, when that happened, he'd think of me.

I doubted it. I, on the other hand, have thought of him nearly every day since. He has certainly been important to me over the years. A tarot-card reader once told me that the rape enabled me to break away from my family. I thought it was a ridiculous thing to say, but I suppose it's true.

Keeping the Rape a Secret

When I was raped, I didn't feel I could tell my parents what happened, so I washed out my bloody panties and kept quiet. A few days later, I was ironing a shirt when my mother asked me what was wrong, because it was apparent something was wrong—but even then I didn't say anything. Four months later I left for college, having told no one but a teacher and a guidance counselor. (Actually, I didn't even really tell the counselor. When I came to the part I couldn't bring myself to say, the counselor supplied the words: "And then he got a little rough." Even in my confusion, that seemed like an understatement. And that's as far as it went.)

After I left at 17, I never lived in my hometown again. When I returned for short visits, I rarely left my parents' house. I felt as uncomfortable and vulnerable as I did when I was 16. But that was another gift my rapist bestowed—agelessness. Because I think so frequently of that night in April 1980, my teenaged self is still strong inside me. Because of my rapist, I'm forever young.

I've always called him "my rapist," mostly because I don't know what else to call him. Whenever I use the phrase, I think I should find another one. I don't want to say his name, though, and no word I can come up with conveys what I think or feel, so I just go on calling him "my rapist."

Seeing my rapist's engagement photo that day triggered a fantasy in my mind, one I'd never had before. I told myself that if I ever actually saw my rapist, I would have no trouble killing him, especially if all the legal and karmic rules were somehow suspended. (It was a fantasy, so I got to make that bargain.)

I told myself that even all these years later, I was still entitled to hurt my rapist. I'd never held a gun for longer than a few terrifying seconds, but in my fantasies I had a rifle.

And then I had another fantasy. I imagined calling him up and telling him what an effect he'd had on my life. I imagined the right combination of strength and bullying in my voice.

For months after I saw the photo, I kept thinking something might be gained by calling him. But as time went by, the idea seemed so filled with drama and tension. In the end, I think I chose not to call my rapist for the simplest of reasons: I didn't want to talk to him.

Dealing with the Memories

In the years since, I've gone on dealing with my rape as before—sorting through it with friends, burying it under new experiences. The way I think about my rape will probably go on changing. I don't know if I'll ever be "done" with it. It's always incredible to me when I hear people talk how forgiveness enables a person to move on. Over the years I've actually felt the memories of my rape dulling, and for that I am grateful. But forgive? Please.

What I can say is that I stopped reading my hometown newspaper. And the only time I think about guns now is when deer season opens and my neighbors fill the woods and meadows with their shooting.

But sometimes I still think about how I would have begun that call: I would have used the phrase all old acquaintances use: "Remember me?"

I Want to Give Others Hope

Rachel

Early on, Rachel recognized peculiar behavior in her boyfriend, but chose to overlook it or make excuses. She now realizes that she was manipulated by an abuser. She also acknowledges that she suffered from posttraumatic stress disorder as a result of her abuse. Many rape experts believe this is a very common reaction to sexual assault. She left her boyfriend to protect her children and found she also saved herself in the process.

My meeting with Paul was really just a typical boy-meets-girl beginning. I was an eighteen-year-old single mother. Initially, there was no attraction for him, but I developed one. He was good looking and very funny. He moved in with me.

I didn't know what early warning signs were at the time, but boy, if I had known then what I know now! He was overwhelming at first, courted me with roses, charm and passion. But he was terribly possessive, and didn't like me talking to other men, and had a sort of strutting, stereotypical masculinity. He could be very crude about women at times, and I found myself constantly justifying him to family and friends.

The violence started, as I now know it does, with name-calling, which graduated to pushing and hair-pulling. It eventually became violent battery. I was ashamed, and covered the bruises. I feared him, but I also pitied him. I didn't know that he used his story of a terrible childhood to manipulate me. All I saw was an abandoned child.

The story of how the sexual violence began is more fully told on my website Aphrodite Wounded. But it was just something that I thought was not real because he was my partner, even though it hurt. Also, I believed I deserved it.

Rachel, "Rachel's Story," *Hidden Hurt*. www.hiddenhurt.co.uk. Reproduced by permission.

Many friends left me because I would not leave him. Desperate to hang on to the few I had left, I started to lie and say he was not hurting me, that he'd changed. In six months, I was not the young woman he'd met. Life depended on keeping him happy so he wouldn't hurt me.

At first, I believed him when he said he was sorry, and that he would change. I started to not believe it after a while. But by that time, I was terrified. I fully believed he was capable of killing me (he did go on to murder a male).

The sexual violence seemed to utterly despoil all my fantasies of loving and being loved. He would sometimes tell me I was a stupid, prudish bitch who needed a good f---; he seemed to enjoy desecrating my highest ideals. I wondered if they were worth hanging on to.

I didn't know what to be to stop it; it didn't occur to me to think it was strange that sometimes he said he was doing it because I was a whore, and at other times, because I was a prude. I now know that it was not about anything that I was or was not. It was about him. At any time, I was never permitted to say no. Strenuous refusal met with beatings.

But you know, I never stopped thinking about escape. While I was busy telling him that yes, I was looking forward to marrying him so he didn't beat me bloody, I was secretly looking for a way out. Being honest about leaving meant beatings, violent rape, death threats. I tried to leave several times; once I got the police to come and get him out. The lady across the road persuaded me to take him back.

Of course, I sometimes felt that I loved him too. . . .

Protect the Children

The clincher came when I could see what the violence was doing to my little boy, who was becoming more and more withdrawn. I couldn't have it. I had had a child by Paul, too, and I could not have her growing up with it. I didn't know then, as

I do now, that I was also worth being free for. I actually made arrangements to be evicted from the flat I lived in.

I told Paul that as soon as I could find somewhere else, we'd move back in together. That was not true; I had no inention of doing that, but did not dare say so. I moved in with a friend. He still came every day, still beat me when we were alone. But eventually I made the break . . . when others were about.

I was stalked, raped again and threatened, emotionally blackmailed. I got a court order. I came out so sick, so depleted. I was hospitalized for severe depression; what I now know was PTSD [posttraumatic stress disorder].

But I clawed my way back. I met and married my current partner, who, because of Paul's crime of murder, adopted my baby girl. I went to university because I wanted to get professionally qualified to help other women who'd experienced what I had. Funny, I thought I was "too stupid" to succeed, but I achieved consistently high results.

It's been a hard slog. I wasn't to understand, until I was in the middle of writing a literature review on marital rape, that the sexual violence, which still sat in me and shamed me so badly, was absolutely real; that all those feelings I'd had (and which are shared at different parts of Aphrodite Wounded) were valid. I kept stopping writing to cry and shake as it all came back. . . .

Rape by Partners Is Real

I got sad, and then I got mad. I saw what the view of rape in relationships tends to be, and that invalidation certainly did not fit my feelings. I asked myself: what if the feelings of women raped by partners are actually what is real, and not the invalidating views? I knew I'd found truth in that.

I came to understand that I hadn't made him do it—he'd wanted to keep me down, and had known that raping me was a good way to snuff out any rebellion.

I decided I would equip myself with all the knowledge I could on rape by partners, so I could reach out to others and let them know that they are not alone, and that there is healing for them. It hurts me that women experience this in aloneness.

I am a laughing, clever, warm, loved and loving woman who survived. I still have my moments, but I did survive, and in the words of my friend, Jes, I now thrive.

I want others to know they can too.

CHAPTER 3

Preventing Date and Acquaintance Rape

Sharing My Story Makes a Difference

Katie Koestner

Katie Koestner was the victim of a sexual assault when she was an eighteen-year-old virgin in her third week of college. Despite her protestations and forceful objections, her date raped her. She spoke out against rape early on, appearing on the cover of Time *magazine and becoming a national antirape spokesperson. She explains that she tires of telling the story over and over, but is spurred on by those who share their stories with her. She says, "My activism did not emerge from the physical rape alone, but from the whole of the experience, the night and the days that followed and continue to follow."*

When Koestner explains her mission of informing young people about sexual assault, she offers a concise and apt definition of date rape: "My most basic goal is to help students understand that rape is no longer a crime of force alone, but also one of consent."

Sharing my story with students took me to over a dozen colleges by the time I graduated, and I have decided to continue this crusade. I intend to go to graduate school eventually, when my "peer educator" status expires. Currently, I work from campus to campus (college, high school, and military) not only as an educator, but as a catalyst for change. My goal has never been to show up for a couple of hours, speak, and leave, but rather to reach as many people as possible, leaving ideas, enthusiasm, and inspiration behind.

Change means going beyond awareness, moving from theory to practice. My most basic goal is to help students understand that rape is no longer a crime of force alone, but also one of consent. Though state laws still vary in their definitions of sexual assault, I believe we are moving toward this more respectful interpretation: that the burden is on the initiator of a sexual interaction to obtain some clear form of consent before proceeding.

Is this an attempt to challenge biological destiny? That is the question I ask myself as I have traveled from school to school speaking to men about rape. Men seem to disagree on the answer. I was told at one school that, "Well, no means no, up to a certain point. Let's call it the point of no return. Then she can start kicking and screaming, but it doesn't matter because she's taken me that far, now it's too late." Or another man: "If she teases me and then says no, I'd jerk off all over her," quickly followed by, "Katie, you're trying to change biological destiny—you know Darwin, survival of the fittest—men just have to spread their seed around."

Fortunately, comments like these seem to be getting slightly less common as I continue my activism (thank God). Is this real progress, or are men just more savvy about keeping their comments between themselves and "the boys"? The real question is, Do fewer comments translate into fewer sexual assaults? Theory to practice. On occasion a high-schooler will state that, "Guys can always control themselves; it doesn't hurt that bad." Or another admits that he can tell "when a girl has had enough" (somewhat less encouraging), or a rare brave individual will challenge a roomful of his peers about sexism or harassment.

Approaching the Male-Female Issues

Ultimately, I am not challenging biological fact, but rather social stereotype and traditional gender roles. For hundreds of years women have been expected to resist sex, and to protest so as not to appear too eager. Men have been taught to read these signals as "maybe" and thus to proceed with whatever convincing it takes to change a woman's mind. As a result, some women are playing by these rules and some women are playing by the new rules that obligate a yes to mean yes, a no to mean no, and maybe to mean maybe. Every day that I speak, I see confusion over the current rules under which the dating game is being played. Male students are afraid to ask permission out of fear of rejection. They are unsure how they should go about communicating. Some men are worried that they will be accused by a vengeful woman even if they do everything "right." Women still feel trapped by the no-win labels of "slut/tease/prude."

By far the most dramatic changes in attitudes have come from my "He Said—She Said" program. I tell my story first, and Brett Sokolow, my cofacilitator, speaks on alcohol, responsibility, and communication. After the lecture portion we divide the entire audience into single-sex groups and facilitate discussion around various realistic scenarios of student sexual interactions. The scenarios are challenging enough that they require more than a simple analysis, which engages the audience and heightens the level of debate.

The students begin their discussion by framing comments and opinions in terms of "Todd" and "Amy," the characters from the scenarios (yes, this is heterosexist), but move on to "I" statements rapidly. I believe this transition produces the self-examination that leads to behavior change. I hear the strongest endorsement of clear verbal communication and respect toward women from the men after these programs. Meanwhile the women benefit from a forum of empowerment and a chance to voice their differing opinions on "risk reduction." After the breakout sessions we invite students to a coed postprogram forum where they talk to each other.

Analyzing the assumptions made about levels of sexual interaction and how one arrives at each enables the students to dispel rape myths. I recall a male student who finally understood that one level of sexual interaction does not necessarily translate into a green light for the next level. At the beginning of the program he said that he could not understand why a woman who was bold enough to perform oral sex on a guy when he asked for sex would not therefore be able or likely to voice her discomfort with vaginal penetration. By the end of the workshop he stated that he would get verbal clarification from future partners.

Sometimes I think that it is one thing to teach students the definition of rape, but entirely another to get them to understand what that definition means. That is the advantage of the breakout sessions, as opposed to the lecture format. For example, you can tell students that having sex with someone who is incapacitated because of alcohol or drugs is against the law, and they will nod in agreement. However, when you then ask them who is responsible if both parties are incapacitated, or how drunk is "incapacitated"—there are a hundred different responses. Other points of contention are the difference between "seduction" and "coercion," or "How much of a threat is a threat?"

To illustrate, I will often tell the story of a high school tenth-grader who said, "I asked her nineteen times, and every time she said no, but the twentieth time she said, 'Fine, get it over with.' Is that rape?" Even after hearing my story (during which I explain that I was asked and said no at least a dozen times), some students will say that the twentieth time she gave consent. Only upon further discussion am I able to show them that consent needs to be a freely given agreement and mutually understandable to both parties, and that context matters.

Working on Programs and Policies

Changing the attitudes of students is only half of my mission. I also work with the administrators, staff, and faculty at schools that will permit me to meet with them. Having now visited nearly every state, I have found a wide range of approaches to the problem at different schools. In my opinion there is no perfect school. There is no school without rape, no matter how Catholic or Mormon, no matter how liberal or conservative, no matter how rural, no matter how few students are enrolled.

There is also no one school that is doing everything possible to stop sexual violence from happening or to deal with it when it does. Some schools have good policies in their handbooks. Some have good resources in the form of rape crisis centers in their communities for rape victims. Some have great orientation programs and dedicated peer educators who even get work study or academic credit for their endeavors. Some have well-trained, extrasensitive police forces or security. Some have great proactive people in high administrative places. Some have dozens of bluelights, safety walks, low hedges, well-lit walkways, and doors that are never propped open. Some have campuswide sexual assault response protocols, sexual assault response coordinators, and sexual assault task forces—with members who *all* attend on a *regular* basis. And so on . . . Some have a combination of the above. No one is perfect.

Our knowledge about the issue is rapidly developing, and lawsuits and criminal cases are producing new precedents for risk management guidelines. Those schools that think they are doing "everything possible" are as vulnerable as the woman who thinks that she is smart and responsible and will never be raped.

I visit some schools that fall into that top echelon of proactive approaches, who still do not have their "Sexual Assault at XYZ University" materials written in a "victim-friendly" manner. Rarely is there enough information on why paper bags should be used to take clothing worn at the time of the assault to the hospital for a rape kit, how much the kit costs, how to get transportation to the hospital, and who might come along as a support person. That's just one example.

Many campus "What to Do If . . ." brochures do not list the hours when you can call resource phone numbers, or whether or not those resources are confidential. Sometimes the schools have only the brochure, and little or no information in the handbook itself. But the handbook, in many ways, is the "safest" place for a victim to turn, because she doesn't have to go asking for the "SEXUAL ASSAULT BROCHURE," and most students already have a copy of the handbook. If she is seen reading it by her roommate or a friend, it doesn't automatically mean that she was raped. These are just a few of the ideas on victim sensitivity I try to share with college administrators.

Federal Guidelines Should Help

Fortunately, if nothing else, there are mandatory federal guidelines for the bare-bones approach to sexual assault on campus. The Campus Security Act of 1990 and the Sexual Assault Victims Bill of Rights were both passed in the last ten years and give some minimal direction to schools.

Yet are all the colleges even complying with these basic minimum rules? No. I visited one university last year where the school used to have a sexual assault policy, and then it was taken out. Why? Because, as the vice president (who informed me that he had been in higher education for longer than I had been alive) said, he has seen handbooks grow thicker and thicker over the last thirty years, and the incidence of sexual assault has not decreased in the least. I asked him if he thought that we should discard our state laws on murder and other crimes as well, since those crime rates hadn't significantly decreased. At another school I encountered an administrator who believes that the solution to the sexual assault problem on college campuses today is to make sure that there is a chair in every single dorm room, because sex never happens on chairs. Another dean said that there is no sexual assault at his institution—in fact, "There isn't any sex here period—this is a Catholic institution." Denial and cover-up.

Are most schools like this? I can't speak for "most," because I haven't been to most. There are certainly too many, though. As with the students, my goal is also to inspire administrators to change their views on this issue. I recognize that I cannot change everyone. I cannot assume that because an administrator is a man, he will not be receptive, or because she is a woman that she will be sympathetic. In fact, in my experience often the older female administrators are more difficult to work with than the men. I imagine that they have won difficult battles in what has been traditionally, and still is for the most part, a male-dominated profession. I am sure some women perceive addressing the issue of sexual assault as addressing a "women's issue," and if they become known as supportive of "women's issues," they will not be taken seriously by their male colleagues on other issues.

Change Does Come

The good news is that many of the schools that I work with do change. I find out months after my program that they have developed a Men Against Rape group, or that the administration has incorporated my suggestions on consent, or ideas from my book, into their college policy. Sometimes I hear that the school has created a sexual assault response coordinator position and started development of a protocol checklist system for the members of a campus sexual assault response network. Most change results from student activism and actual incidents of sexual assault (and sometimes the lawsuits that come out of the incidents); more than the federal guidelines, these things are what seem to propel the not-so-proactive college administrators along. Sometimes I encounter students or staff who are lower in the "chain of command" and are needing that extra push from an outsider to get the attention of the "decision makers" at their campus. They know that by bringing me to campus, their voices and efforts will be validated by someone with "authority" from the outside.

High schools, mainly private boarding schools, and especially private boarding schools that used to be all male, concern me the most. I have visited about two hundred high schools, and most of them are private schools. Many public high schools refuse to discuss sexual assault, including my own alma mater. High schools do not have to follow any federal regulations regarding the rights of sexual assault victims. High schools rarely focus on more than sexual harassment issues, if that, despite the occurrence of sexual assault. There are fewer lawsuits against private high schools for sexual assault issues. The students, because they are young, often do not have the support or the understanding of the issue necessary to try to make changes. Private schools are even more vulnerable than many colleges to public scandal, because they are smaller and have insufficient resources to weather the storm of a "big" rape case. One woman student told me that one night she was drinking with some other students in a dorm room in the boys' hall. She thinks something was slipped into her drink. When she came to, she remembers that there were about a dozen boys in the room surrounding her, and that she didn't have any clothes on. She vaguely remembers being carried to another room, but also remembers different guys on top of her. What was done about the incident when she reported it to the head of the school? She and one of the boys were suspended for a couple weeks for violation of the alcohol policy. When I confronted the administration, I met with a wall of denial.

So are attitudes really changing? Is there less rape? Some studies purport that peer education on sexual assault issues is having little to no effect on long-term attitudes and behaviors. If I believed these findings, I would quit my mission. I believe in change. I believe in going beyond awareness to the emotional, sensitive root of the issue. I believe in small miracles, one at a time. Like when the members of a fraternity at one school—whose five brothers had yelled "Hey ho, hey ho!" and "What do we want, lots more date rape!" at the women who passed by fraternity row during their Take Back the Night march—came to my speech and then stayed afterward to speak with me and the women whom they had offended and angered. I explained to the president of the house that although their harassing comments did not necessarily mean they were rapists, they fell squarely on the "continuum of sexual violence." This concept, although familiar to those of us who have ever taken a women's studies class or read any of the literature on sexual violence, was not one that made any sense to him, until I explained it. I believe that hearing my story of rape, representing one end of the continuum, enabled him to be willing to understand the relationship between what happened to me and the comments that were made from his fraternity porch. Unfortunately, I think most of the time it is the personal story of one person, not the horrific statistics, that compels students to look for the relevance of my message in their own lives.

Another small miracle was the letter of intense apology and remorse written to a woman by her rapist. He had realized from my speech that what he had done was indeed rape and decided to write to her in an attempt to bring her some healing and closure. He did not expect to "make up" with her, or to get anything in return.

Every day that I tell my story is one less day that "he" has power over me. It is one more day that other survivors can see there is someone else out there who will not wear her rape like a scarlet *R* on her chest for others to scorn. It is one more day that I will hear stories of rape and renew my hatred of statistics because of the faces behind them. It is one more day that college administrators will be asked to reexamine their policies and protocols, and question whether they are doing everything possible on this issue. It is another day that a survivor's voice will shatter silence. It is one more day toward a day without rape.

We Should Fight a "War on Terror" Against Rape

Kristen Bain

Kristen Bain passionately presents the goals of the women's center on her college campus and emphasizes the importance of educating both men and women about rape in a variety of ways. She stresses that the women's center antirape activists want to remain "visible, vocal, and vigilant."

I find it extremely ironic to be discussing rape culture in a time of a supposed "War on Terror." It amazes me that our government can spend billions of dollars "protecting" us, and "fighting for" us, its citizens, against the so-called "Axis of Evil," but I can't even get a permit to sell pepper spray on campus at wholesale. Why? Because girls could use it in a "vengeful manner." You know, in an argument or something, to retaliate. The liability, we are told, is just too great.

Pardon me, what did you just say? You said that giving the womyn [an alternate spelling of women used by some feminists] on campus another outlet to defend themselves is too great a liability? Okay, just wanted to be clear on that.... Because we are not allowed to sell or distribute pepper spray to campus womyn, they are forced to find their way to one of the local mega-stores and fend for themselves (pun intended), paying inflated prices, supporting corporate giants—if they remember to buy it at all. Young college womyn often suffer under the delusion "it won't happen to me."

To combat this problem, we at the campus womyn's center are begging businesses on a nearby campus corner to carry pepper spray at a discounted price. So far, only one of the twelve businesses we have approached has agreed.

Kristen Bain, "Rape Culture on Campus," *off our backs*, vol. 26, no. 2, September 2002, pp. 9–10. Copyright © 2002 off our backs, inc. Reproduced by permission.

Andrea Dworkin [the feminist writer who has argued that there is a link between pornography and rape] describes rape as an act of terrorism and the ultimate affront to humyn dignity. She says that not only is rape a barbaric crime of power and hate, it is THE most effective method of perpetuating the patriarchal system. Not only does rape exert power, it terrorizes and intimidates and then works to shame the victims in order to keep them quiet and non-confrontational. Rape is no benevolent dictator. Rape is an evil despot placed at the helm of a patriarchal society and reinforced every time it is used as a weapon in the war against womyn.

This war is fought with increasingly steep repercussions on my college campus every semester. Those of us who speak out are denounced, personally attacked in newspapers, sent hate mail, sneered at in the food court and, my favorite, accused of instilling a "victim mentality" in womyn in order to secretly perpetuate the very patriarchal systems of oppression we claim to fight against. In essence, we are accused of "working for the enemy." While it's a laughable accusation to those of us in the know, I shudder to think of wide-eyed freshwomyn listening in terror as the evils of feminist agendas are described to them.

Education Is the Best Tool

Attacks against our center and me are nothing new and are not effective. Lambasting our efforts is an exercise in futility. We're certainly not deterred from our mission and never will be, especially not now, in this time of "War on Terror." The time has never been more right to take up arms against those who would harm us again and again, with their actions, their words and their attitudes. Education is the best tool on college campuses, and that is the primary instrument in our struggle.

Our university has celebrated Rape Awareness Week for several years now, with varying levels of success. The turnout is always much higher if there has been a well-publicized incident on campus near that time. Unfortunately, incidents that happen weekly are not so well publicized, especially when it comes to athletes as perpetrators, or we might have a better showing every year. That one single week during the entire year was devoted to educating the campus about the epidemic of rape. When we stopped to consider why we weren't more effective in our efforts, the answer was clear: one week out of the year wasn't nearly enough time to carry out what we needed to do. We proposed monthly programming to the then-coordinator of our center and were granted permission to do what we felt would be most effective.

To this end we have developed plans to speak at mandatory dorm floor meetings at the beginnings of every semester. During our presentations, we'll hand out materials about safety and information about the women's center, along with stats, facts and figures. We're hoping something catches their attention, and then if they are assaulted, they'll know what to do about it and who to call.

We plan to sponsor speakers from Planned Parenthood and the DA's office as well as police officers to teach basic safety routines. We host a self-defense workshop twice per semester, and have found an outlet for our discounted pepper spray.

Addressing the Issues of Power and Control

The problem I have with these programs is that it puts the responsibility on the victim and doesn't actually address the root of the problem at the heart of rape culture: why men rape. The issues we want to examine are those of power and control. The question we want to ask is, What can we do to PREVENT rape, rather than merely teaching our campus womyn whom to call when they are assaulted. How can we help to change the perceptions and attitudes about womyn and subsequently about rape, on our college campus?

The answer seems to lie again in education. We are speaking to the men's floors in the dorms, as well as to the womyn's. Our coordinator visits the fraternity houses and does workshops and presentations about what "no" really means, and how to understand when sex is inappropriate. We try to put a face on the subject of rape by utilizing the services of a volunteer who is also a rape survivor. She speaks openly about the attack, that her attacker was a football player, and how the assault has affected her. She is a compelling speaker and is always met with great respect by her audiences. We set up information tables on campus to distribute facts and figures. We get the number of womyn students on campus each semester and divide it by 4 (1 in 4) and post that number (those who will be the victim of rape or attempted rape) in big red numbers on a banner at various events on campus. It is a sobering figure. We plan to stage a demonstration to illuminate the 1 in 4 statistic.

Our most viable strategy has been and will remain to be as visible and vocal as possible and to inform our classmates as to what rape really is. In addition, we must continue to be vigilant in our stance against those anti-feminists, who decry our position and who work to perpetuate the myths that have built rape culture into the edifice it is today. We will continue our struggle to educate others about the attitudes and myths that have allowed womyn to become objects, and why objectification causes rape. Enlightenment about rape culture is never easy, but it is a task that we can never afford to let lapse, especially not now, in light of the current "War on Terror." We are using that phrase to our advantage, to teach others about the War on Womyn, using rape as an act of terrorism, that has been going on for centuries . . . although somehow I doubt it's what [President George W.] Bush had in mind when he exhorted us to "watch out for" our neighbors.

How I Became an Antirape Advocate

Michael Scarce

In 1989 Michael Scarce was raped. He tried to resist his rapist, but was afraid to call out for help or engage in a struggle that might be overheard because of the environment of hostility toward homosexuals that existed on his campus. He hid the experience for many years and only came to grips with it when he began course work and research on rape and sexual violence. In his work as an activist, he has sought to increase awareness of same-sex rape as a societal issue and to address the needs of adult male survivors of sexual assaults.

In the autumn of 1989 my friend Tom and I returned from summer break to begin our sophomore year at Ohio State University. We unpacked our belongings and settled into room 332 on the third floor of Bradley Hall, an undergraduate residence hall in the south area of campus. Each of the four floors of Bradley Hall was divided into two wings—one for women and one for men. Eve Wing had its own bathroom shared by the thirty-some residents living there. The rooms were not air-conditioned, and the dining hall food was less than stellar, but we were glad to be back on campus. The majority of the thirty-two men sharing our wing were first-year students, and they were equally as excited to be out on their own for the first time in their lives.

The return of students to campus ushered in a flurry of activity as Welcome Week programs and parties abounded around us. Tom and I had been elected president and vice president, respectively, of the Gay and Lesbian Alliance, our

Michael Scarce, "Male-on-Male Rape," *Just Sex: Students Rewrite the Rules on Sex, Violence, Activism, and Equality,* edited by Jodi Gold and Susan Villari. Lanham, MD: Rowman & Littlefield, 2000, pp. 39–42. Copyright © 2000 by Jodi Gold and Susan Villari. All rights reserved. Reproduced by permission.

campus gay and lesbian organization. We held weekly meetings and organized events while striving to increase membership and politicize the organization's activities. As GALA became more visible throughout autumn quarter, the organization and its officers frequently appeared in the local media, promoting GALA and challenging homophobia on campus. As our visibility increased, so did our Bradley Hall floormates' recognition that their two neighbors in room 332 were gay.

The stares and sneers from our thirty floormates began early in the academic year and slowly escalated to verbal abuse, menacing, and death threats. Messages were left on our answering machine, death threat notes were mailed to us, signs saying "Die Faggots" were posted on our door, and as the intensity of the intimidation increased, so did the frequency. Eventually the third-floor men's wing became so dangerous for Tom and me that the university was forced to evacuate everyone, relocating the male students and splitting them up across campus before someone was bashed or killed.

Tom and I were moved to a nearby Ramada Hotel, where we lived in adjoining rooms for the last few weeks of spring quarter. Both of us were escorted around campus by an armed security guard hired by the university to protect us in the midst of hostility. A protest of more than three hundred students erupted on campus soon thereafter. Some students applauded the university's relocation decision while others criticized campus officials for "pandering" to gay activists. Still others blamed the university administration for allowing the situation to escalate to a level that necessitated such drastic action. The third-floor men's wing of Bradley Hall remained vacant, sealed, and empty for the remainder of the academic year. A media frenzy ensued, with coverage from CNN to the *New York Times*. This year was devastating for me as I struggled to survive in such an environment of hostility, humiliation, and degradation. I lived in constant fear and frustration while the weight of the events took its toll on my academic performance, my relationships with family and friends, and my health.

The Encounter

However, the pain and violation I experienced during those months before the relocation exceeded the incidents of homophobic harassment. During winter quarter of that academic year, Tom went home for a weekend visit and I was left alone. I was nervous about what could happen to me, what those men could do to hurt and punish me. It was a weekend in February and I decided to go dancing at a gay bar downtown to get out from under the suffocating weight of it all. I went alone, expecting to meet up with friends. The music was great, the bar was hopping, and I was having a wonderful time. As I danced, I noticed a handsome man standing at the edge of the dance floor. He watched me for the duration of several songs and smiled when I returned his stares. Later we talked and I learned he was from out of town, visiting Columbus on business. After an hour of conversation and heavy flirting, I invited him to return with me to my residence hall to escape the loud music, crowd, and cigarette smoke.

On returning to my room and continuing our conversation, we grew more physically intimate with each other. We were on my bed and began to kiss. Slowly he attempted to unzip my pants, and when I resisted, he became surprisingly rough. The more I pushed his hands away, the more aggressive he became until finally he used force. I asked him to stop but was too embarrassed to raise my voice for fear that others next door or outside in the hallway would hear what was happening. I was afraid the men who hated me for being gay would use this situation as one more excuse to bash me. After several attempts to unfasten my jeans, he finally succeeded and yanked down my pants and underwear. What happened next is somewhat of a blur. I remember he forced me to lie on my stomach and climbed on top of me. He shoved his penis into me, without lubricant and without a condom. He held me down as I squirmed and fought, suppressing the urge to vomit. The physical pain ... worsened as he continued, and I began to cry. Soon thereafter I stopped moving in hopes he would just finish and get off me. Eventually he did stop, pulled up his pants, and left without saying a word.

The walls in Bradley Hall were very thin. The air vents in the doors were so large you could hear practically everything through those wide cracks, and many of my neighbors were home that night. One yell, one shout would have attracted the attention I needed to stop what was happening, but I could not bring myself to cry out. What would my floormates think? They already hated me for being queer, so how might they react if they responded to my cries for help and burst in on that lovely scene—a man on top of me, penetrating me? There was nothing I could do except lie there and go numb.

After he left, I took a long shower, standing under the water and crying. The smell of him was on my body, his semen was between my legs, and I washed with soap over and over—lathering and rinsing continuously. I endured some minor rectal bleeding for the next day, and remained sore for many more. I did not contact the police or visit the hospital emergency room. I did not seek counseling or formal support, nor did I confide in any of my friends for several years. I was ashamed and embarrassed by what had happened, identifying the experience as a form of bad, regretted sex.

The Realization

It was not until a year later that I began to make more sense of my experience. Through my academic course work in OSU's Department of Women's Studies, I took an internship with the university's Rape Education and Prevention Program, where I conducted library research on rape and sexual violence. Gradually I came to terms with the fact that I had physically and mentally resisted that night a year ago in Bradley Hall and that I had been, in fact, raped. I now blame those thirty floormates for my rape as much as I blame the man who assaulted me. They created and shaped a space, both actively and through negligence, in which I was gagged, effectively silenced, and unable to resist. Their intimidation weakened my spirit, lowered my self-worth, and forced me to appropriate a victim mentality that impeded me from regaining control of my life.

So very little has been published on the rape of adult males. As I began to search for documentation that resonated with my own assault, I was dismayed at being unable to locate many scholarly articles or even popular, first-person accounts of this form of sexual violence. Slowly, over the last few years, I have collected what scarce writing and research have been published about men raping men. Although I was raped by a gay male acquaintance, I discovered multiple other forms of same-sex rape between men—rape in prison institutions, assault by strangers, gang rape, and more.

The Crusade to Help Others

As my knowledge and understanding of the subject has grown, so has my interest in speaking and educating others about this form of sexual violence. When I speak publicly and conduct sensitivity trainings on male rape, I relate to others the story of my own assault, for it serves as a highly useful illumination of the ways in which homophobia and other forms of oppression create climates that foster and perpetuate rape behavior. My rape in Bradley Hall was simply a microcosm of the broader rape culture we all live in, a culture that encourages and condones sexual violence wielded as a tool for the subordination and control of those with less power in our society. Scores of male survivors have approached me after speaking engagements or contacted me later to share their own rape stories with me.

As I gradually became more involved in antirape work on campus, I began facilitating sexual assault workshops for the Rape Education and Prevention Program in classrooms, residence halls, student organizations, fraternities, and sororities. My involvement continued through graduate school, and after receiving my master's degree I was hired as the full-time coordinator of the program. My transformation from helpless victim to empowered survivor has refashioned my sense of self and purpose in life. The atrocities I have experienced provide a lens through which I am better able to see the complexity of injustices around me, and I have learned to harness the resulting anger in positive and productive ways that fuel my drive for social change. I wonder if the man who raped me realizes what he has created.

Drugged and Raped

Tammy Ivar, as told to Sandy Fertman

At age 15, soon after breaking up with her 18-year-old boy-friend, Dan, Tammy got an unexpected call from him. After agreeing to go see his new apartment, she was victimized by Dan and his friends. Drugged with Rohypnol, Tammy was raped re-peatedly. She recalls that night as well as the difficulty of facing her friends and family, going back to school, and, finally, speaking before Congress to promote the Hillory J. Farias and Saman-tha Reid Date-Rape Drug Prohibition Act of 2000. Placing two popular date-rape drugs in the same class with marijuana and heroin, this legislation gives courts the power to aggressively punish those who carry, deal, or use the drug on others.

One Sunday in June, I was hanging out with my friend, Jessica, when the phone rang. It was my ex-boyfriend, Dan, and I was psyched to hear from him. When we broke up, we promised we'd still be friends, but it hadn't been easy to make that transition from boyfriend to buddy. He asked if I wanted to come over and check out his new apartment. I would have asked my parents, but they didn't want me hanging out with Dan at all because he was 18 and I was only 15. I lied and told them Jess and I were going over to her house. We left, walked to the end of my street and waited for Dan to pick us up.

I hadn't seen Dan in months. When he pulled up, he had a creepy looking guy named Jeff in the car with him. I had a bad feeling about Jeff right away, but Jessica and I were so into going out that I just ignored it. We were both like, "Cool. We're hanging out with two older guys."

The Closet

When we got to Dan's place, my feelings about Jeff were confirmed. He immediately whipped out a joint and lit up. Jessica and I just sat there while Dan and Jeff got high. I'm sure they thought we were goodie-goodies, but I didn't care. Then Jeff opened this closet to show us a whole shelf covered with pounds of pot in plastic bags and pills in containers. I think he thought he was impressing us. He said the pills were called "roofies" and that they made you forget everything that happens while you're on them. I'd heard about them in health class so I was pretty freaked.

For a second, I wondered why they had so many drugs around. Then it hit me: Dan's roommate was a drug dealer. I was bummed that Dan had changed so much since we went out. I kept thinking about what my parents would think if they knew where I was. Then I asked Dan to drive us home—I didn't want to be there anymore. He said he would, but that he needed to do a couple of things first. I waited and waited. Finally, I asked Dan if I could use the phone, and I called my older sister. I talked to her for a few minutes, but I didn't tell her where I was. I almost asked her to come and get me, but I was worried that my parents would find out.

At around 4 P.M., another guy, Sean, showed up, and Dan said Sean could take me home. He looked about 19, was attractive, and seemed like a nice guy, so I figured he was reliable enough to get me out of there. Everyone was annoyed that I kept nagging to leave, so I decided to sit on the couch until Sean was ready to go. Dan asked, "Do you want something to drink?" I said, "Sure." He gave me a Mountain Dew in a big plastic cup.

Where Are My Clothes?

The next thing I remember was waking up in a strange bed—and I wasn't alone. There was a guy in bed with me. It was Sean, the one who was supposed to give me a ride. I felt like I was in a weird dream. I had on a T-shirt and shorts, but they weren't mine. I thought, "Where am I?!" My head was cloudy. Someone was talking to me. It was Dan, begging me to wake up because my mom was on the phone.

When I didn't come home the night before, my parents called the police. They found me because of my call to my sister who, luckily, had caller I.D. Dan gave me the phone, but I was so out of it. I had no clue what had happened. It was as if one whole day just disappeared.

My mom told Dan to bring me home immediately. Jessica was still there, too, and she helped me get out of the bed. Dan, Jess and I walked outside, and this woman from the office of the apartment complex stopped us in the parking lot and asked, "Are you Tammy?" When I said yes, she said, "Your parents are on their way." My parents had called the apartment building as soon as they found out where I was. They also called the police.

It Hurts to Walk

When we went inside the office to sit down, I realized that I was hurting all over and had terrible pains in my genital area. It hurt to walk, but it also hurt to sit, I didn't know why or what had happened to me down there. When my mom and dad showed up, I knew I was in big trouble by the way they looked at me. I was sitting between Dan and Jessica and they were elbowing me to sit up straight. Dan whispered, "Please stop looking like you're drunk!" He was really scared, but I just couldn't wake up.

The police arrived right after my parents. Dan stood up and took them aside. I didn't hear what he was saying, but my mom did. He admitted that he and his friends had drugged Jessica and me with roofies and had sex with us. My mom grabbed me and said, "We're going to the hospital NOW!"

Meanwhile, the police kicked through Dan's apartment door to arrest Jeff and Sean. They found Jeff flushing roofies down the toilet and arrested him for possession of drugs. Dan wasn't busted because he ratted out his friend. It's called a plea bargain—something that I think is totally gross about our legal system.

The Rape Kit

At the hospital, I felt completely confused. I couldn't see straight or think clearly. I felt like I was having a nightmare but I couldn't wake up. The police detectives started questioning me in an accusatory way about how I ended up at the apartment. They asked me how many drinks I'd had and what kind of drugs I'd been doing. They said one of the guys told them I'd had six beers!

It wasn't until one detective said the word rape that I realized how serious everything was. I remember thinking hard: Did someone have sex with me? I had a flashback of Sean's face hovering over me, and then I remembered waking up next to him. I put it all together: the pain I was feeling, the fact that my clothes were gone. As the fragments of memory washed over me, I was horrified.

The hospital had to do a procedure called a "rape kit" on me. This is where they examine every inch of your body for rape evidence, including your clothes. In fact, they sent me home in scrubs so they could test what I had been wearing for evidence. Going through that invasive testing was really hard, both physically and emotionally. I was in so much pain and I didn't want nurses touching me, especially down there. I felt nauseous and hungry because I hadn't eaten in over 24 hours. I was still in a haze. The doctors gave me a pill so I wouldn't get pregnant, tested me for drugs and STDs and did an AIDS test, which truly terrified me. It made me realize that being raped could literally kill me.

"That Girl Who Was Raped"

I slept for a full day once I made it to my own bed. When I woke up the next morning, I still felt woozy. What had happened to me was starting to really sink in. I had been drugged and raped—over and over again—by a man I didn't know. My parents were loving and supportive, but I couldn't deal. I felt so ashamed and embarrassed, I could hardly look at my own body. I stayed in the house for months. I hid in my room and didn't talk to any of my friends. I didn't even come out to watch TV because my story was constantly on the news.

I felt so stupid for getting into that situation and I blamed myself for the rape. If I hadn't gone to that apartment it never would have happened. I got so depressed, my parents finally took me to a psychologist, and I was prescribed antidepressants. That summer was the darkest period of my life.

Then it was time to go back to school. I was so scared to see people because I thought everyone now regarded me as "that girl who was raped." It took a lot of courage to walk into school, but nobody teased me or mentioned what happened. Even better, an old friend came back into my life that semester. Seeing her again was like a fresh start. Her friendship helped me feel more confident.

As for Jessica? I spoke to her over the summer, but I felt really uncomfortable because I was still so embarrassed. I wanted to forget everything, but I was also a little confused about her. On the day of the rape, she didn't seem upset. And I'd heard that she was friendly with Jeff—the guy who had supposedly raped her. It just didn't add up. I didn't feel like I could trust her anymore.

Justice for All?

Sean and Jeff were going to trial that fall, but Sean—the guy who raped me—fled the country by changing his name and moving to England. The trial was postponed until the police could find him and bring him back.

While we half waited, and half went about our business during that fall, my sister died suddenly of heart problems. My family and I didn't care about the trial anymore. We just wanted to grieve. But as the months went by, my sister's death gave me strength to push forward. When they finally found and shipped Sean back to America, the prosecutor called us. Now I was ready to see my rapist pay for what he did. I said, "OK. Let's take him to court."

The first day of the trial was terrifying, especially when Sean was led in to the courtroom. He was quickly found guilty and sentenced to 21 years in jail. I thought, "I'll never have to see him again." But after an appeal, the rape charge was dropped because of "insufficient evidence." Even though there was a lot of physical evidence that he had had sex with me, I couldn't remember the details of the rape. It made me mad to learn that charges are often lowered—or dropped alto-gether—in rape cases where drugs or alcohol are involved. I felt terrible, but at least he was given a five-year sentence for his drug offenses.

It wasn't until after the trial that I finally understood that Dan's original phone call was a setup to drug and rape me. My mom refuses to let me speak to Jessica anymore since she believes she was involved from the beginning. Honestly, I'm suspicious, too, since medical tests showed that Jessica had not been drugged. But I've never learned exactly what happened. In a way, I think it's better not to know so I don't have to re-live it. And I hate to think of another girl allowing me to be raped, especially a friend of mine. But, I'll admit that not knowing the truth sometimes leaves too much room for my imagination.

Making a Difference

When I turned 18, I thought I had really put my rape behind me. I had a great boyfriend, I graduated from high school, and my life felt on track. Then, in March of 1999, someone from Washington, D.C., called asking me to speak as a victim before Congress. They wanted my testimony to help pass a bill that would make it much harder for criminals who drug and rape girls to get off easily, like Sean did. My mom said to me, "You'll be making history." I really wanted to go, although I was a little scared to speak in front of so many powerful people. Before my rape, I was sort of shy. Now I would have to be brave.

I sat on a panel with police officers and rape counselors and spoke to Congress. When I saw the TV cameras I was nervous, but also really happy. A group of molestation and incest victims were sitting behind me during the testimony, all between the ages of 12 and 16. Many of them came up to me afterward and said, "Thank you so much for doing this." They looked up to me because I spoke out! I was no longer a rape victim. I was a hero. It was such an amazing feeling.

Because of my testimony, legislation was passed stiffening jail sentences for anyone who uses drugs to rape someone. The bill is called the Date-Rape Drug Prohibition Act of 2000, and it was signed into law . . . by President Clinton. In the end, what happened to me helped a lot of girls because I wasn't afraid to tell my story. I realized that the only way anyone can create something positive out of rape is to come forward. It's so important to prosecute—for yourself and for society. It also shows rapists what can happen.

It's all too common for a victim to think she did something to make a person violate her, but the reality is the victim is not to blame. No one has the right to rape or do anything to you that you don't want them to even if they use drugs or alcohol to lower your inhibitions. Only you have control over your own body.

Watch Yourself

Signs you or a friend has been doped with roofies or another "date-rape" drug:

- Appears intoxicated, even if sober

- Loss of coordination

- Slurred speech

- Extreme drowsiness, sedation

- Confusion

- Memory loss or blackouts of an 8- to 24-hour period of time

- Nausea, vomiting

Protect Yourself

- Never leave your beverage unattended.

- Never accept open-container beverages from anyone except a server.

- When going to parties with friends, make a pact to watch each other's beverages and to leave together as a group.

- If someone shows symptoms of ingesting a date-rape drug, call 911 and seek medical attention immediately.

The Date-Rape Drugs:

Rohypnol: A potent tranquilizer that causes sedation in 20 to 30 minutes. It has no taste, no odor, and no color. Street names: Roofies, Roach, R-2, Mind Erasers, Rib, Rope, Forget Pill.

GHB: Causes intoxication followed by a deep sedation. It is odorless and colorless, but tastes salty. Street names: Grievous Bodily Harm, Liquid G, Cherry Meth, Easy Lay, Gamma.

Ketamine: A fast-acting anesthetic used most commonly by vets during surgeries on cats and dogs. It is tasteless, odorless, and colorless. Street names: Special K, Ket, K, Vitamin K, Kit Kat, Keller, Cat Valium, Purple C.

Organizations to Contact

The editors have compiled the following list of organizations concerned with the issues debated in this book. The descriptions are derived from materials provided by the organizations. All have publications or information available for interested readers. The list was compiled on the date of publication of the present volume; the information provided here may change. Be aware that many organizations take several weeks or longer to respond to inquiries, so allow as much time as possible.

An Abuse, Rape and Domestic Violence Aid and Resource Collection (AARDVARC)
606 Calibre Crest Parkway, Suite 103
Altamonte Springs, FL   32714
e-mail: aardvarcinfo@aol.com
Web site: www.aardvarc.org

AARDVARC is a nonprofit organization of volunteers dedicated to combating family and relationship violence, sexual violence, and child abuse. Its Web site includes a Sexual Violence menu with topics like "After Sexual Assault," "Healing," and "Male Victims." These sections list related books as well as online information. The "Resources by State" section provides links and phone numbers to other centers and organizations.

Gift From Within
16 Cobb Hill Rd., Camden, ME   04843
(207) 236-8858 • Fax: (207) 236-2818
e-mail: JoyceB3955@aol.com
Web site: www.giftfromwithin.org

Gift From Within is an international nonprofit organization for survivors of trauma and victimization founded in 1993. It provides support and information to trauma survivors struggling with posttraumatic stress disorder and other traumatic stress syndromes. The Web site provides tapes and DVDs to order and online articles in more than twenty categories, several having to do with sexual assault.

Men's Rape Prevention Project
P.O. Box 57144, Washington, DC   20037
(202) 265-6530 • Fax: (202) 265-4362
e-mail: info@mencanstoprape.org
Web site: www.mencanstoprape.org

The mission statement of the organization states that members "mobilize male youth to prevent men's violence against women, . . . build young men's capacity to challenge harmful aspects of traditional masculinity, to value alternative visions of male strength," and see themselves as "allies with young women and girls in fostering healthy relationships and gender equality." They sponsor the Men of Strength (MOST) Club in high schools and colleges, a multimedia public education campaign, and strength workshops and training. The Web site offers a calendar of nationwide events and a blog.

National Center for Victims of Crime
2000 M Street NW, Suite 480, Washington, DC   20036
(202) 467-8700 • Fax: (202) 467-8701
e-mail: webmaster@ncvc.org
Web site: www.ncvc.org

The Dating Violence Resource Center offers free downloads of studies, surveys, and articles about the subject. This resource center offers a hotline that serves victims in more than 180 languages. The Violence Against Women section offers online articles on several topics, including rape-related posttraumatic stress disorder, dating violence, and help for teens, with tip sheets available on various aspects of assault.

National Sexual Violence Resource Center (NSVRC)
123 North Enola Dr., Enola, PA   17025
(877) 739-3895 • Fax: (717) 909-0714

e-mail: resources@nsvrc.org
Web site: www.nsvrc.org

The National Sexual Violence Resource Center (NSVRC) is an information source for data on all types of sexual violence; articles, booklets, and guides are available on its Web site. NSVRC publishes a semiannual newsletter, *The Resource*, and coordinates an annual national Sexual Assault Awareness Month in April.

National Teen Dating Abuse Helpline
(866) 331-9474 (hotline)
Web site: www.loveisrespect.org

The National Teen Dating Abuse Helpline Web site is a source for teens offering links to other Web sites, information on recognizing abuse, toolkits of resources for promoting awareness of teen dating abuse, a blog, and a helpline staffed by trained peer advocates. The site features an online Teen Dating Bill of Rights and publishes the *Real Love* e-newsletter.

One in Four [formerly The National Organization of Men's Outreach for Rape Education (NOMORE)]
P.O. Box 6912, Williamsburg, VA   23188-6912
(757) 221-2191
Web site: www.oneinfourusa.org

"One in four college women has survived rape or attempted rape. Statistics can change, men can help." One in Four educates men about rape and offers presentations, training, and technical assistance to men and women to prevent rape.

Rape, Abuse, and Incest National Network (RAINN)
2000 L Street NW, Suite 406, Washington, DC   20036
(202) 544-3064 • Fax: (202) 544-3556
e-mail: info@rainn.org
Web site: www.rainn.org

RAINN is an anti–sexual assault organization that provides information on prevention, recovery, and prosecution. It operates the National Sexual Assault Hotline, a partnership of more than a thousand local rape treatment hotlines that give free, confidential services. The Web site offers a list of local crisis centers, upcoming events and programs, and news on public-policy issues.

Speaking Out Against Rape (SOAR)
817-A Virginia Dr., Orlando, FL   32803
(407) 898-0693 • Fax: (407) 898-0721
e-mail: info@soar99.org
Web site: www.soar99.org

SOAR runs educational and prevention programs to empower survivors of sexual violence and to enhance public understanding. It offers emotional and financial assistance to victims. The Web site contains a section on reflections and inspiration, and a resource section with online articles, such as "What to Do If a Friend is Raped" and "A Rape Victim's Rights." There is also a list of links to Web sites of organizations, activists, and survivors.

For Further Research

Books

Vicki Aranow and Monique Land, *Journey to Wholeness: Healing from the Trauma of Rape*. Holmes Beach, FL: Learning Publications, 2000.

Jeffrey R. Benedict, *Athletes and Acquaintance Rape*. Thousand Oaks, CA: Sage, 1998.

Susan Brownmiller, *Against Our Will: Men, Women and Rape*. New York: Simon & Schuster, 1975.

Patricia Easteal and Lousie McOrmond-Plummer, *Real Rape, Real Pain: Help for Women Sexually Assaulted by Male Partners*. Ormond, Victoria, Australia: Hybrid, 2006.

Lori B. Girshick, *Women-to-Women Sexual Violence: Does She Call It Rape?* Boston: Northeastern University Press, 2002.

Scott Johnson, *Man to Man—When Your Partner Says No: Pressured Sex and Date Rape*. Brandon, VT: Safer Society Press, 1992.

George B. Kehner, *Date Rape Drugs*. Philadelphia: Chelsea House, 2004.

Me Ra Koh, *Beauty Restored: Finding Life and Hope After Date Rape*. Ventura, CA: 2001.

Scott Lindquist, *The Essential Guide to Date Rape Prevention: How to Avoid Dangerous Situations, Overpowering Individuals and Date Rape*. Naperville, IL: Sourcebooks, 2007.

Aileen McColgan, *The Case for Taking the Date Out of Rape*. New York: Rivers Oram Press, 1998.

Tamra Orr, *Frequently Asked Questions About Date Rape.* New York: Rosen, 2007.

Lori S. Robinson, *I Will Survive: The African-American Guide to Healing from Sexual Assault and Abuse.* Emeryville, CA: Seal Press, 2002.

Peggy Reeves Sanday, *A Woman Scorned: Acquaintance Rape on Trial.* New York: Doubleday, 1996.

Clare Tattersall, *Date Rape Drugs.* New York: Rosen, 2000.

Vernon R. Wiehe and Ann L. Richards, *Intimate Betrayal: Understanding and Responding to the Trauma of Acquaintance Rape.* Thousand Oaks, CA: Sage, 1995.

Robin Warshaw, *I Never Called It Rape: The* Ms. *Report on Recognizing, Fighting and Surviving Date and Acquaintance Rape.* New York: Harper & Row, 1988.

Periodicals

Melissa Abramovitz, "The Knockout Punch of Date Rape Drugs," *Current Health 2, A Weekly Reader Publication,* March 2001.

Camilla Cavendish, "So We Are Weak on Rape? Think Again," *The Times* (London). February 1, 2007.

Ruth G. Davis, "How to Talk Your Way Out of a Date Rape," *Cosmopolitan,* December 2000.

"Life After Rape: A Victim's Tale," *The Gazette* (Montreal), September 2, 2006.

Renee Moreton, "Spiked Drinks," *Youth Studies Australia* 22, September 2003.

Kathleen Parker, "How Guys Are Victimized," *Cosmopolitan,* September 2007.

Felicia F. Romeo, "Acquaintance Rape on College and University Campuses," *College Student Journal,* March 2004.

Suzanne Smalley, "'The Perfect Crime': GHB Is Colorless, Odorless, Leaves the Body Within Hours—and Is Fueling a Growing Number of Rapes," *Newsweek*, February 3, 2003.

Laura Sessions Stepp, "A New Kind of Rape," *Cosmopolitan*, September 2007.

Zak Szymanski, "Dangerous Mix: Date-Rape Drugs: Not Just a Straight Thing Anymore," *Curve*, November 2003.

Index